Forgotten Days

Professor F.A. Orhewere

Forgotten Days
Professor F.A. Orhewere

All rights reserved. No part of this publication may be reproduced, stored in any retrieval system or transmitted in any form or by any means, electronic, mechanical, photocopying, recording or otherwise, without the prior written permission of the copyright holder for which application should be addressed in the first instance to the publishers. The views expressed herein are those of the author and do not necessarily reflect the opinion or policy of Tricorn Books or the employing organisation, unless specifically stated. No liability shall be attached to the author, the copyright holder or the publishers for loss or damage of any nature suffered as a result of the reliance on the reproduction of any of the contents of this publication or any errors or omissions in the contents.

ISBN 9781912821891

A CIP catalogue record for this book
is available from the British Library
Published 2021 Tricorn Books
131 High Street, Portsmouth,
PO1 2HW

Printed & bound in the UK

Forgotten Days

Dedication

This book is dedicated primarily to my beloved wife Claris Ermine, who encouraged me especially at our sixtieth wedding anniversary celebration, to record my life experiences as a tribute to the vision of my missionary parents, and also to Almighty God who made it possible.

Romans 8:28 All things work together for good to them that love God, to them who are the called according to his purpose. (KJV)

Contents

THE CALL	7
Chapter 1 WESTERN EDUCATION – A CURIOSITY?	9
Chapter 2 FAITH AND FAMILY	18
Chapter 3 LAND OF MY BIRTH	21
Chapter 4 LIGHT AT NIGHT	26
Chapter 5 FIGHT FOR ENGLAND	28
Chapter 6 PRIMARY SCHOOL IN 1930's NIGERIA	34
Chapter 7 GOVERNMENT COLLEGE IBADAN	57
Chapter 8 CHANGE, CHANGE, CHANGE	79
Chapter 9 GOING TO ENGLAND	88
Chapter 10 LIFE AS A NEWLY QUALIFIED DOCTOR	104
Chapter 11 RETURN TO NIGERIA	108
Chapter 12 FROM COWRIES TO CURRENCY	118
EPILOGUE GOD IS IN CONTROL	120

Introduction

THE CALL

It seems such a long time ago when my immediate older brother and I used to walk along the streets of Uzairue together in the morning, ringing our father's prayer bell in the rhythm of "ding, ding, ding-dong-ding", and shouting in our young voices **"Boys, Girls, come-to-school"**. This routine from Monday to Friday, every week is my earliest recollection of the significance of education in my family for almost as regularly, in the evenings we would overhear Baba, discussing with one or two mature men how to get 'the school' started. We found it curiously exciting. We called out to other children not knowing what the response would be each day to our morning exercise, and at the same time having a strong awareness of our father's hope and expectation.

My father, Baba, was the eldest son of a respected, successful and well-known practitioner of herbal medicine, popularly referred to as a native doctor, in Eme, Ora in the Province of Benin in south-west Nigeria. Today, this region is called Edo State. His father, (my grandfather) had been revered for his knowledge of the practice of divination using the traditional oracle of our people. By tradition, Baba, who had learned the profession, was expected to inherit and continue in his footsteps. However, all this changed when in his late teens to early twenties Baba encountered English and Yoruba missionaries who came to Ora to preach the doctrine and religious philosophy of Christianity. It was the 1890's and they belonged to the Church Missionary Society, an outpost of the Church of England known throughout Nigeria as the CMS Church. Baba embraced and totally accepted the Christian faith wholeheartedly, much to the surprise of his father and the consternation of all the other members of the family. When he told them that as a consequence of his new faith he would want a Christian wedding ceremony when marrying and that they should not expect him to be polygamous (a practice that was widespread then and now, in Ora) it was totally unacceptable to his father. Worse than this, his new Christian beliefs were at odds with the age-old practice of divination. His father tried to persuade him over a number of years to change his position but was unsuccessful and so it was, that some time in the early 1900's, at a date we do not know, that Baba's sustained determination and increasing knowledge of Christian doctrine led him to be baptised; his Christian name was Simeon. In 1906, he married a young woman from another quarter in the village who had accepted his faith and had also been baptised; her Christian name was Mary.[1]

Chapter 1

WESTERN EDUCATION – A CURIOSITY?

The school in Uzairue was in the Mission Compound, along with the church and the homes of the headmaster, some teachers and my father who was the Catechist. A Catechist was the name given by the Anglican church to a trained local evangelist, appointed on their behalf and paid by the Church Missionary Society. Schooling (children going to school) was a new concept in most of the towns or villages that my father was posted to. Most villagers were farmers and needed their children to help them work the land in their farms. Our regular morning bell-ringing exercise was meant to stimulate their curiosity and invite them to release one or two children, to try out this new idea. Sometimes their children would only come to school for a few months or in the seasons when there was less work on the farm. But my father never gave up trying. Getting the community to send at least some of their children to school was an important part of his role.

A typical Mission Compound in those days was a unique and complex small community, centred round the Catechist. He and his family lived in a bungalow which was usually about a hundred yards from the church and on the other side of the catechist's home was the school building. Generally speaking, this was one long bungalow building divided by short walls into classrooms. Close by, there would be a large expanse of land that served as a playing field for games, football, PT and athletics. In the early years of the school, teachers were often taken in and accommodated by church members, but as funds became available, the Headmaster and then the other staff would be housed in bungalows built near the Catechist's home. This was the environment in which I grew up.

After we had our morning bath and had put on clean clothes, my mother would serve our breakfast. Then my brother Edward would call out to me ***"Hurry up Felix or we will be late for school"***, and we would set off on our bell ringing exercise. At first one child or two might come out, and then another one or two. After a few weeks this would grow to a trickle of three, four, or five children sent by their parents to come and find out what school was all about.

School started with prayers and in this way children were introduced to Christianity along with education. Edward being two years older than I, had attained the appropriate age for registration in school. I had not, but as the Catechist's child I was allowed to accompany him to school and sit beside him. I was usually very quiet and did not intrude, until one day when I saw the teacher pick up a cane to hit a boy on the outstretched palm; the boy had been corrected repeatedly but still seemed to be having difficulty with the lesson. Filled with fear, I ran out shouting that the teacher was about to kill the pupil with a 'big stick'. What the villagers' children made of this I do not know but after this experience, I wasn't so keen on accompanying Edward to school. Instead I stayed home and waited for him to get back home when I could ask him what the teacher had taught them, what games and exercises they had played or done and in short, everything they had done that day. By the time the grown-ups considered me old enough to be registered as a pupil, I had learnt not to resent the teacher's corrective measures.

Becoming a school pupil

In response to one question or another, my father, Baba, often told my siblings and I that as he had not had the opportunity to go to school, he might not be in a position to tell us the answer. This made me even more keen to become a school pupil.

One of my older sisters, Grace, liked weaving the locally spun thread which was produced from cotton grown on Baba's farm that all the children helped to harvest. She did not go to school due to ill health in her childhood and early teens. Generally, she wove cloth of different patterns for sale in the local market, but from time to time, she produced a special cloth for making school uniforms like the ones my older brothers, sisters and cousins wore. It was a chequered cloth made from white and dark blue thread. I dreamed of the day when I would be old enough to wear a school uniform too. I was therefore greatly delighted one day when a tailor came to our home to measure me and he was given one of those traditional woven cloths as he went away; after two or perhaps three days which seemed like weeks to me, the tailor came back and I was called to try out my school uniform; I literally jumped into it, almost as if the school was in session and I was late to get there, excited in the knowledge that I was going to become a registered school pupil. The top half was a *buba* with short sleeves and side pockets, while the lower half was a pair of short trousers with side pockets. Once the tailor pulled them on me and fastened the buttons of the buba and the shorts, I ran off to show my new outfit to Baba and my mother, before dashing to the backyard and kitchen to show myself off to my siblings, cousins and the headmaster's domestic staff as well as all the other people in the Mission Compound. It was like a re-run of that day about ten days earlier, when with great excitement I had tried on the new clothes my eldest sister Comfort had made for me, for Christmas. Wearing new clothes is as essential to celebrating Christmas or New Year's day in Nigeria, as all the pomp and ceremony, the church services and the eating.

How soon would school reopen after the Christmas holidays, I wondered! I couldn't wait. This pattern of term time and holiday was something I would gradually have to learn and get used to. After the celebrations and merriment of Christmas and the New

Year, I was duly enrolled as a pupil of St James's C.M.S. School, Jattu in January 1934. We were in Uzairue but this little town in Kukuruku District had three names. Jattu was the name used by the colonial administration in government documents. Uzairue was what we and many people who had come there from other parts of the country called it, while the indigenes called their town Ikpe or Uzairue. I do not remember what transpired on my first day in school or even in the first week or two, but as time went on, it occurred to me that most of the songs and games that we were being taught were familiar, for I had learned them already from Edward. Many of the references and stories that the teachers drew upon came from cultures where education was already established, such as the Yoruba-speaking towns and villages west of the province of Benin and a few were derived from English. This was not unusual because in those days teachers were not expected to draw on the local language and culture of the pupils in order to help them learn, particularly when the local language had not yet been written. Furthermore, as all the teachers had attended teacher training colleges in Yoruba-speaking parts of Nigeria, much of the teaching was in that language. In other towns of Kukuruku District this was not a major problem as Yoruba was widely understood and spoken alongside the indigenous language. But at this time the people of Uzairue spoke their own language and no other. To avoid making the children learn Yoruba first and then English so that they could access primary education, the Mission amended its school policy in Uzairue to introduce the children to the English language and the alphabet earlier so that after spending two years in kindergarten classes, the children could move up to a class where English was the medium of tuition. This class was called Primary Class One. However in their first encounter with western education, the young children of Uzairue found themselves having to learn songs and games in a language they did not speak and words they did not understand. This was not easy. Things were easier when it came to numbers and counting. Counting was taught using numbers from the local language, and therefore children could relate it to what they learned from their parents and siblings at home. I was very fortunate. I was ahead of most of the other children because I had learned a lot from Edward and I had been exposed to Yoruba in the Mission Compound. I had the advantage of speaking Yoruba and English, both of which were widely used in my home in addition to speaking our native Ora language.

All the pupils were boys in the early days of the school at Uzairue because at that time the people lived under a Muslim influence, a religious way of life that was as firmly established there as at Auchi, the District Headquarters just three miles away. This did not encourage the exposure of boys or girls to western education.

Madam Amorettee's campaign for women

There was a lady in Uzairue at that time, an indigene, who wielded a significant influence in all the neighbourhood. She was probably in her mid to late thirties and a socialite. She stood out in the neighbourhood as an activist who encouraged women to be more active in the social, political and business life of the community. She spoke English fluently even though it was pidgin-English, and what that meant to us as little children, was that she must have lived for quite some time in one of the great cities we had heard of, Lagos or maybe Kano. To add to that cosmopolitan image she rode a bicycle but not just any bicycle. It was a ladies' pedal cycle with a curved frame, enabling her to step on or off it quite elegantly. When she met someone she wanted to greet other than by speaking the Uzairue language, she would exclaim in a loud, almost shrieking tone "**Hallo, hawa yuh**?" and then continue the conversation in the local language; if she met someone who asked her in standard English "How are you?", she would reply

"Amorettee". It took us quite some time to make out what this response meant, perhaps a few months, but with the help of older children who understood English better than we did, we finally understood that she was saying ***"I'm alright"***. It seemed quite logical to us from then on to call her "Madam Amorettee", and in all the years we lived in Uzairue, I never did get to know her real name. However, her personal campaign for girls' and women's emancipation was a great help in the drive to get parents to send girls to school. Enrolment of girls was very slow in the first year, but by the following year when the community had seen for themselves that girls were not being corrupted or abused in any way by western education, admissions began to increase steadily although the girls' enrolment always remained well below that of boys. For Baba and the teachers, girls' enrolment was another chapter in a successful 'mission accomplished'.

Language and Identity

The main mission of the CMS was to spread the Christian faith. The church in the small town Uzairue, had been established by my father's predecessor, Catechist Pa Ohiorhenuan, an indigene of a small town near Ora called Ozalla. Although my life up to that point revolved around Uzairue and the Mission Compound, I gradually learned that Uzairue was part of a larger community of towns and villages including Auchi, Agbede, Ibie and others that had been exposed for decades to the Islamic faith and culture which they practised, and had largely adopted Islamic names. Some still followed traditional religions. This group of people spoke variations of the same language but each of the constituent small communities had its own Traditional Ruler.

The Ora communities which my family came from, and the surrounding communities of Iuleha (Uzebba & surrounding villages), Emai (Afuze & surrounding villages), Ozalla, Otuo and related towns and villages lay south of Uzairue and were Christians or practitioners of traditional religion.

This Southern group were later designated as IVBIOSAKON, meaning the descendants of ancestors who indulged in splitting their upper teeth to create a gap between their front teeth to enhance their 'beauty'. The Northern Group, composed of Uzairue and the surrounding communities were designated as ETSAKOR which relates to the same practice but means the people who have for generations indulged in the practice of splitting their upper teeth to enhance their beauty. When I was young, these two groups seemed so different to me, but I later learnt that both groups have in common a history of migrating from the Benin Kingdom during the reign of Oba Ewuare (reigned 1440-1473), and consequently both peoples speak dialects that have their roots in the language of the Bini people (Edo). Interestingly, while the speech of the people of the Northern group could easily be understood by an Ora person the reverse was not true, and it was not uncommon to see an Ora person using gesticulations and hand signals in an attempt to communicate.

Early church in Uzairue

On Sunday mornings, the church bell was rung two times with an interval in between of about half an hour, the first was to remind listeners that it was a day of worship and that they were to come to church, and the second time was to inform all present that the worship service was about to commence, usually within five minutes. The order of service was rather condensed because every statement had to be translated and repeated in the local language so that the congregation could understand and be part of the worship. However there were only a few copies of the Holy Bible, the Hymnal Companion (combined hymns and the order of worship and prayers), and the Yoruba Hymn Book, all personal copies owned by members of the Mission Compound and a few congregation members. Bookshops in Auchi and some market stalls stocked some of these books. Yoruba was just about understood and reasonably spoken even if it was hotch-potch in some villages. Communication was therefore the major problem, but this was dealt with slowly and successfully by the grace of God rather than by man's cleverness or planning.

One Sunday afternoon, in the course of an outdoor preaching in place of the evening service, I remember the procession stopping beneath a shady tree where quite a number of people were relaxing, some smoking tobacco in pipes made from the hollow bamboo and a clay pot, some drinking palm wine, others playing 'Ayoh', and one traditional healer attending to a client. Baba, my father, preached to all who cared to listen to him for about ten to fifteen minutes, and must have then noticed the traditional healer and walked up to him, stood still and watched him throwing the strung cowries for divine consultation so as to advise his client. After about two minutes of watching the healer performing his rites and advising the client, Baba suddenly shouted **"No, no, no"** to the healer saying to the hearing of every one that the healer had misinterpreted the oracle and was giving the wrong advice to the client; there was silence for a while, and the shocked healer asked Baba what he knew about the oracle and its interpretation, to which Baba replied that he had been in that profession for a number of years before he gave it up on becoming a Christian. Baba then proceeded to explain the correct interpretation of the oracle as well as what the remedy was; moreover the cure did not require the client to procure any white cock nor tubers of yams; nothing more was required from him than the fee already paid for consultation. Everyone was amazed and dumbfounded and kept silent until the healer said to his client **"Well, Baba has told you everything and so you can go home now"**. All of a sudden, the crowd that had gathered and all the Christian congregation applauded and went on clapping their hands, saying **"Baba, you do well oh, Baba, you do well oh"**. Shortly after that, prayers were said and the procession made its way back to the church singing songs of praise to God. Arriving at the church, closing prayers were said and the congregation dispersed. For a long time, many of us in the Mission compound, especially the younger ones, were flabbergasted and wondered that Baba was so well versed in the art of the traditional oracle as well as its interpretation. For me and my siblings, Baba made us wonderfully proud on that day and for a long time to come.

Some years later, I visited Uzairue to spend some time first of all with my older sister Mercy and her husband Joseph Erhukpe Omoikhudu when he was the Headmaster of the CMS School and on another occasion to spend time with my brother Henry while he was Headmaster at the school in the nearby village of Awuyemi. [4]

The progress that had taken place in education in the Estako Community by that time was wonderful and almost unbelievable. In Uzairue as well as in the surrounding towns and villages, there was a proliferation of schools and the attitude of the ordinary man or woman towards western education had changed radically. There was no longer any need to plead or persuade the average family to allow their children to go to school, irrespective of their religious background. Indeed, when I recounted the bell ringing that my brother Edward and I had undertaken only fifteen years earlier, they would look at us in astonishment. It sounded to them like fiction. Those days were gone, gone, gone and had been forgotten.

Chapter 2

FAITH AND FAMILY

Baba absorbed the doctrine of Christianity with great enthusiasm and, in order to fully understand it all, he first learned Yoruba and later English by private tuition. The Yoruba language had been introduced to Ora people following the Ogedengbe inter-tribal wars when, like many other tribes in the neighbourhood, some Ora indigenes had been captured and taken away to Ilesha and other Yoruba towns. Some years later, when many of them regained their freedom they returned to Ora, speaking Yoruba and practising Yoruba customs; many had even acquired Yoruba names and this became fashionable as evidence of being "westernised" and therefore "civilised". It was in the spirit of this trend that Baba assumed the name **AJAKAIYE**, the family name by which we, the children, were all known and registered in school until the year 1938 when my father publicly and legally reverted to **ORHEWERE**, as it had been in previous generations. Baba had mastered the Yoruba language even to the extent that he could read the Bible (in Yoruba) well and explain and teach people the doctrines of Christianity. After recognising his talent, devotion, and determination, the CMS authorities did not hesitate to send him for formal theological training in Ondo in 1908, where he became a trained and certificated Catechist, Grade 3. Years later in 1924, he was sent to St Andrew's College, Oyo to do one year's theological training. This was Nigeria's premier institution for the training of both clergy and teachers at that time. He qualified as a Catechist Grade 2. These courses constituted the only formal educational training he received throughout his life.

These opportunities enabled Baba to consolidate his knowledge of Yoruba, written as well as colloquial and idiomatic. He had also become reasonably fluent in English, without going to formal school. His informal education was entirely driven by his faith in God. Baba worked as a missionary in Ora District for nearly two decades gaining a lot of experience. It was common at the time for indigenous CMS missionaries to be moved to a new posting every few years. Baba established several new churches. Seeing that church growth in Ora and the growth of schools linked to these churches was reasonably assured, the CMS sought to put the missionary service of Baba and Mama to use further afield.

Life as a Christian in those early days was not always smooth-sailing, and in some of their postings, Baba and Mama experienced difficulty and even threats to their lives and the lives of their children, all of which were ascribed to wickedness, hatred, envy and jealousy, as well as witchcraft. However, their faith in God through Jesus Christ was strong and unwavering, and they endured and survived, and overcame their difficulties. Members of the communities that they lived in, also called them Baba and Mama because of their fatherly and motherly nature and love shown to everyone.

Life became more stable, predictable and comfortable from year to year for Baba and Mama, and their family steadily increased in number. They were blessed with children in the different locations they were posted, starting with Comfort the eldest, born in Ora, Grace also born in Ora, Alfred born in Uzebba, Henry and Mercy born in Esan. Shortly before Baba's transfer from his second posting to Uzebba, he was blessed with a baby boy named Edward. Two years later in 1928 while my parents were in Okpe, I was born and named Felix.

My eldest sister Comfort, pregnant and approaching term, came from her matrimonial home to reside with Baba and Mama until her delivery; by mid-July 1928, she was safely delivered of a baby boy who was named Albert. A few weeks later, and returned home.

Chapter 3

LAND OF MY BIRTH

Mission Compound in Okpe

Life in the Mission Compound in Okpe was generally orderly, quiet and in its own way exciting. The day usually began with hearing Baba's hand-bell ringing for about ten seconds for prayer. Often some of us in the family were already awake to undertake the morning chores, like sweeping the compound and going to the river nearby to fetch water to ensure there was enough to use for that day; this was done by my older brothers and sisters, while for me, I could sleep on. When I was about three years old, I joined the family in morning prayers. Any other member of the Mission Compound community, my cousins who lived with my father, the teachers, and strangers passing by were welcome at Baba's morning prayer session. A hymn was usually sung in Yoruba but whoever spoke and understood English was welcome to sing the English version; copies of The Hymnal Companion were always available. This was then followed by a reading from the Holy Bible. Baba usually followed the reading with explanations and/or comments; sometimes he asked some of us questions to ascertain that we had understood the reading and what lessons should be learned. Then followed the prayer by Baba or anyone he chose. It all lasted about thirty to thirty-five minutes. After morning prayer, the children, supervised by Mama, went about their various daily assignments of sweeping the inside of the house (all the rooms), sweeping the outside open spaces around the house, fetching water from the river for drinking and washing, washing any inadvertently unwashed plates and cooking pots from the night before. These children included my siblings, relations who resided with Baba or with the teachers, and any servants, whether house boys or house girls or housemaids. Fully grown adults were not involved in these morning schedules of duty; they were usually informed when bathing water had been placed ready for them in the bathrooms, cold or hot (usually warm really) according to the season of the year.

The terrain of Okpe was hilly and undulating and immediately behind the Mission House where we lived was a huge rock, perhaps better described as massive really, about twenty to thirty yards from the back of the house, and about the size of a big bungalow. I can still visualise it as it was when I was age one and a half to two years. It was great fun as I grew and could walk, to be assisted by my brother Edward, to climb the sloping face of the rock, holding on to some shrubs deeply rooted in its crevices, and then to endeavour to slide down, experiencing quite a bumpy glide!

Rumbling in the sky

One morning when everything was calm as usual, the headmaster came out of his house and excitedly called "children, children, children, come out!" We all stopped whatever we were doing, young and old, and even toddlers, and rushed the front garden of his residence, wondering what it could be that the headmaster thought was necessary for us all to come and see; a few passers-by walking along the motorable road about twenty yards in front of the living quarters of the Mission Compound also stopped and paid attention to the excited figure of the headmaster, more out of curiosity I believe. The sun had come out well above the horizon; there was no rain cloud in the sky and yet there was a rumbling sound up in the sky quite different from the sound of thunder which was the only sound from the sky that was familiar to us. The headmaster shouted to the little crowd that had gathered, "look up everybody and you will soon see something, looking like a very big bird, flying across the sky but its wings do not move like an ordinary bird". I was about three years old and I was curiously excited and wanted to know what it could be that was about to intrude in our generally quiet life pattern. The overhead sound was more like a motorcycle requiring good servicing, a sound we were also familiar with, and it was getting louder, coming from the cloudless sky. We all looked up, anxious and attentive, and then, it appeared slowly and fortunately in the western part of the sky so that we did not have to look directly into the sun. As it moved across the sky, we saw this mass with side appendages high up, and looking more like a cross, viewed from underneath. **"That is an aeroplane"** said the headmaster, as we all kept looking. It obviously was the origin of the rumbling motor-cycle sound, and although it did have a resemblance to the shape of a bird, the wings were rigidly in place and did not flap. The 'bird' in the sky was visible for about a minute and after it had disappeared from view, the 'rumbling in the sky' could still be heard for another minute, and then we all suddenly seemed to wake from a trance and started speaking to one another. The headmaster also began addressing us all, telling us that the object we saw in the sky was about the long dimension of three heavy load lorries joined together head to tail and could carry as many as forty to fifty people at the same time; the marvels of white men and science! I knew nothing called science at the time and neither did the bigger boys and girls, and I am sure many of us did not know the very word 'science'; the headmaster obviously would know because he was very knowledgeable; after all, he knew enough to teach even the teachers who taught all the schoolchildren things they did not know. For some months after, any time there was thunder we wondered if another aeroplane was flying by. Many years later, I learnt that such flights in remote areas like Okpe and other towns and villages in Kukuruku, as well as other parts of Nigeria, were used for aerial surveys of the country to compile data for comprehensive and accurate information about Nigeria, perhaps also including surveys for mineral deposits. I sometimes asked myself "How could anyone up there in an aeroplane detect with apparent accuracy the location and identity of specific mineral deposits deep under the earth's surface"? Curiosity and more curiosity about knowledge was piling up in me as I grew older.

Appetising Pounded Yam

In Okpe there was a church already in existence and Baba was assigned the task of building up the population in the congregation from a pagan community, as well as establishing new churches in the surrounding villages. There was also a school with a good complement of teaching staff, and Baba and the Headmaster planned to cooperate and jointly develop the school, and to found new schools in villages beyond a reasonable walking distance from Okpe town.

Baba was in his fifth year of service in Okpe when my younger sister Florence was born in 1932 and a few months later, Baba was transferred to Uzairue.

Years later, in 1939 and 1940 when Edward and I were pupils at the school in Igarra just six miles away from Okpe, we frequently went to spend weekends there with my big brother Alfred who was a teacher at St Paul's School, Okpe. Baba and Mama were no longer stationed at Okpe at that time.[3]

It gave us special pleasure whenever Alfred took us to visit families and friends who were very close to our parents when they were at Okpe; they received us with great joy and happily recalled that I was born there. The highlight of those visits was usually on Sundays after morning service when at least one of these families would invite us to lunch, telling my big brother not to fail to bring us. When we arrived for lunch, we were usually served sizzling hot pounded yam with melon seed soup (egusi) and chunks of "bush meat". I have not gone back to Okpe for decades and the life pattern may have changed, but in those days, "pounded" yam was not "pounded" in a mortar, or made in a pot from powdered yam. It was cooked, then crushed and ground on a big slab of a grinding stone; how the person grinding the yam still kept it hot beats my imagination. I looked forward to those visits because I, and I am sure, all of us enjoyed those meals. In Ora and most of Nigeria where pounded yam is eaten, the cooked yam is usually crushed, pounded and turned over and over in a large mortar with a heavy pestle. *"Okpe, oh Okpe, land of my birth"*.

Baba and Mama were re-posted to Okpe nearly two decades after they had left and served there until their final retirement from missionary service in the early 1950's.

Chapter 4

LIGHT AT NIGHT

The provision of artificial light played a significant role in the growth and development of both the church and the school as established by the Church Missionary Society in those days. There was no public supply of light by gas or electricity as we learnt was the case in many advanced countries. In our society in the 1930's, artificial lighting in the homes which was usually only at night was by traditional methods. In communities that produced oil from the fruit of the palm trees, the thrash obtained after squeezing the oil from the exocarp of the boiled nuts was dried and kept for producing light as required later. An alternative was to use the palm oil in a shallow metal or clay pot with a wick; the clay pot was rather cumbersome to hold, so the metal pot with a handle was preferred. Another traditional method of lighting whether indoor or outdoor that was common was to use $2^{1/2}$ foot long strips of a special dry tree trunk which, when lit in a fire, burned slowly but with a bright enough flame to give a bright light over a large area; this method was unfortunately prone to accidents. With increasing western influence and trade, many more people had access to a large variety of imported kerosene lamps that gave many people a feeling of being progressive but neither the lamps nor the kerosene was cheap. There was also the gas lamp, which was a pressurised kerosene lamp that had a mantle that when lit gave out a lot of heat as well as a very bright light that could light up a wide area; this was the ultimate in lighting in those days, more often used in social functions but not in church because it was expensive. When a church could afford it, or if a church member could afford it, gas lights were used on special occasions such as Christmas Eve, and New Year's Eve worship services.

The Mission Compound in every one of the stations where Baba was posted served as a haven for pupils who found our home inviting as well as conducive to learning or doing their home-work. We had light from one of more of the sources I have described. Moreover, in my family, we discussed and assisted one another in solving home-work questions, in preparation for the next day's school work. Another thing that attracted other pupils to the Mission Compound was the opportunity to improve their spoken Yoruba or English through conversations we had.

Chapter 5

FIGHT FOR ENGLAND

In Otuo

Just as Baba and Mama had a baby girl shortly before moving from Okpe to Uzairue our family was blessed with another baby girl, Mabel, in Uzairue a month or two before Baba was transferred to Otuo early in 1936. The way of life generally in Otuo and the social outlook were remarkably different from Uzairue. Ethnically the indigenes were closer to the Ora people and a significant number of them were already Christians. Islam was virtually unknown and not practised in Otuo but traditional religion was widely accepted and practised. The colonial administration preferred to write the name as *Otwa* as did all members of the community in my primary school days. Otuo clan is a large community established in twelve villages (Otuo n'igbeva, originally in Ora language as *Otu n'igbeva*) who in the days of inter-tribal wars and communal clashes, had settled in strategic locations on rocky terrain and hill tops for safety. These twelve settlements were linked by footpaths some of which required dexterity in hill and rock climbing to negotiate. I remember vividly how I had difficulty trying to do it by myself, slipping and falling sometimes, only to be saved by an older person holding my hand and hauling me up; yet adults managed it confidently, and even carried bulky and heavy farm produce or market wares on their heads; in addition to these the women often had a baby on their backs. I was eight years old and I suppose that if I had grown up in that environment I might have become adept at it years earlier and would have been able to negotiate these paths on my own. Going up, difficult as it was, seemed to me easier than coming down, because if you were careless coming down, you could crash and fall in a direction that was highly undesirable, like a gully. Yet these rocks conferred the advantage that the indigenes made use of several generations earlier, and ensured their safety from surprise attacks and invasions! However, some decades before my father was posted to Otuo, the colonial administration brought general safety to the area and many people had migrated from the hills to the plains, with some of the villages becoming linked by motorable roads.

The church and school were located between Ighera and Iyeu, along the main motorable road, in a mainly level plain about a hundred to two hundred yards wide, surrounded by dotted hills of good farmland. The other side of the main road had the teachers' quarters, on slightly sloping ground. Behind that was a range of undulating hills and I remember that on one of those hills, about half a mile further out, was an isolated house. I was fascinated by it, and together with other children made an exploration to find out more about it. From the main road passing by the school, a branch road turned off and up the hill, a motorable road, to that very isolated house, a bungalow; the surroundings were clean, and had well maintained hedges and flower gardens. It was the government "Rest House" and was kept and maintained by a non-resident staff made up of the cook, the steward, and the gardener, who lived in nearby Iyeu and Ighera.[Sketch 1]

War and Duty

The Rest House was used from time to time by the District Officer (generally referred to as the D.O.), a white colonial officer, who came to live there for days at a time, in the course of duty. During those few days, there was intense activity in the community which as a child I did not understand; there were people going to and from the Rest House virtually all the time. One thing I did understand was that shortly after the D.O. came, a long bamboo pole was planted in the garden if the previous one had fallen down and had rotted away or had been eaten by termites; a string (so I thought) would be tied to the top of the pole with one end sticking out about six inches above the end of the pole, while the rest of the string was anchored to the edge of the roof before disappearing into the house. No sooner this was done than some sound came from the house of talking, singing, or playing music. I later learnt that the sound came from a box called a radio and the string was the aerial which brought the sounds from far away to the box. With the other children I would crawl towards the house in the evenings between about 5 and 6.30 pm to listen to the radio. If the D.O. saw us, he would shout at us to go away and we would run off only to return after a few minutes, when he had disappeared into the house. After all, we meant no harm, and he must have come to the same conclusion after a day or so but thought it better and safer not to appear to encourage us to get too close to the house. It was from the D.O.'s radio that we had confirmation late in 1939 that a major war had started in Europe. Some of our teachers later told us that the German leader Adolf Hitler wanted to rule the world, and he had therefore invaded the countries adjoining Germany for a start. We were familiar with the geography of the map of Europe and thought that Hitler's war was far away from England, especially as England was separated from mainland Europe by sea. It was therefore quite a surprise to me, when in a matter of a month or two from the beginning of Hitler's war, our government mounted a campaign to recruit young and able Nigerians into the army as part of the West African Frontier Force. Many homes and families in Nigeria had been affected by the 1914 - 1918 war, either directly as men who joined the Army, fought in The Cameroons, died in the war front and never came back, or indirectly from an outbreak of a terrible disease like consumption or influenza which killed many people over the same period. We later learnt that this disease which became known as Spanish Flu had spread round the whole world. But in Nigeria it was widely believed that it was caused by the poison gas used by Germany in an attempt to conquer the world because their military efforts were being steadily overpowered by the combined efforts of the rest of the world. Notwithstanding all that experience from the earlier German war, many Nigerians still joined the army "to fight for England" in the new World War that started in 1939.

The Entertainers

It was in Otuo that I came to know about the world-famous entertainer Charlie Chaplin. At intervals of about three to six months, a local entertainer would arrange to have it announced in the marketplace, in the school, in the church, and by the Town Crier, that he would be coming shortly to entertain people with his 'magic lantern'. He duly arrived and in the evenings, and when many people had gathered in the village centre, he would set up his magic lantern half covered with a piece of black cloth, while a white sheet of cloth was set up on the wall about two to three yards away from the lantern. He then collected money from the crowd, whether one penny (locally known as a kobo) or two pence or even three pence (known as toro, *anglicised pronunciation tore-raw*) per person I do not remember, and then he would start his gadget; to my surprise, images appeared on the white cloth on the wall... and that is how was introduced to Charlie Chaplin, the great pioneer movie star of the Silent Films era. All the children and I believe most of the adults found these magic lantern shows very entertaining. Years later, I found out that in the cities such as Lagos, Ibadan, Kano etc there were cinema houses that showed films that were more sophisticated than our magic lantern shows. It cost the audience sixpence (also called sisi) if standing or two shillings & sixpence if seated.

Another highlight that I remember from about the same period was a travelling photographer, Alabi, who like the magic lantern man, did the rounds from one village to another every few months, encouraging people to have their photographs taken for the payment of a moderate sum of money. Each visit was an exciting event for us and we learnt that he had been a soldier, and fought with the British troops in The Cameroons in the 1914-1918 World War. Our interest and excitement was heightened when he explained that he went to war well-prepared and fortified with traditional medicines and incantations, so that bullets fired at him had no effect; he said that in one of the battles at the height of the war, he walked through a hail of bullets into the enemy ranks, and disarmed a Captain (or Commander) of the enemy troops; what was even more fascinating to us was that the Commander was a white German Officer! In those days we did not believe that a black soldier could capture a white officer. According to Alabi, some of the enemy troops fled, throwing away their weapons while the rest surrendered to the British forces. For this gallantry and other brave exploits at the warfront, Alabi was decorated with the DSM (Distinguished Service Medal). This gave him the privilege for the rest of his life of not having to pay the annual head tax that every adult male in the community was expected to pay! What a fantastic consideration and reward by the Colonial Administration! We children would crowd round Alabi after he had finished taking the photographs of those who requested and would ask him to tell us stories about the Cameroon War, which he did with relish, and I believe he saw and appreciated the delight, joy and fascination expressed on our faces. He would then depart for home to return about another six months later after touring and visiting other towns and villages in the District.

In early 1940, Alabi arrived as usual peddling his trade. One adult in the crowd went close to Alabi and asked if he would consider enlisting to fight in the new war against the Germans since he was already well protected and fortified by charms and medicines, but Alabi replied with a smile on his face *"**my brother, two times war no good**"*. We all hailed him, for what I do not know, but the adults in the crowd applauded him for his wisdom. For me and many other children, and perhaps many adults too, that expression "two times war no good" struck a note of firm integrity and wisdom that would live forever in our memories.

As recorded earlier, there was a well-established church, St. Stephen's Church, in Otuo in 1936 when Baba was posted to Otuo. I recall the Baba Egbe, Otuogbai, an elderly man who was the senior of the church elders, friendly, affable, and very much liked by the congregation, young and old. His son was, or became shortly after our coming to Otuo, a catechist, and a few years later, trained and was ordained as a priest in the **CMS** (Anglican) Church.

Chapter 6

PRIMARY SCHOOL IN 1930's NIGERIA

The mid-1930s to late 1930s was a period I remember so well in terms of educational growth and development. My eldest sister, Comfort, lived in Benin City, far far away from Kukuruku District, and every year we looked forward to her coming home to the family for visits that lasted about two to four weeks according to the time of year. We called her Mama Benin as she lived in Benin City; she was also much older than the rest of us, being the first child of Baba and Mama.[2] December visits were fantastic, as this covered the Christmas and New Year celebrations which for us children meant new clothes. And we were like peacocks strutting all over the village streets for weeks, to the envy of poorer children outside the Mission Compound. Comfort was a School Teacher and a successful gifted dressmaker (or seamstress). There was a good old 'original model' Singer Sewing Machine in our home, and whenever Comfort came home, that poor machine went into action almost non-stop, day and night for weeks. There was a large number of requests from the whole household including my father and mother, my siblings and I, our cousins, any servants, as well as other staff and families in the Mission Compound; occasionally people outside the Mission Compound also wanted new clothes and they bought and brought their own cloth. I believe that payments were negotiated for labour in such instances. My father and mother had priority attention and their garments were usually completed within a day; usually a buba with either short or long sleeves, and matching trousers for Baba, and a buba and wrapper with matching head-tie for Mama. What I enjoyed as my contribution to the fiesta was assisting my sister to turn the handle of the machine especially when re-threading an empty spool or spindle; I was fascinated by the ingenuity of the inventors of the sewing machine, both our table top, hand operated model as well as the foot pedal model that I had seen in shops and market stalls. If anyone had mentioned an electric sewing machine in those days, I would have been so bewildered, considering it as the biblical dream of Joseph that would most likely take decades to come to pass. I had vaguely heard of electricity only as a wonderful means of producing light by remotely pressing a button, and it was only available in very large cities like Lagos, Kano, Ibadan, or Port Harcourt.

When Mama Benin took a break from this 'fever and high pressure' of dressmaking, she would talk to us, the children, about Benin City and her teaching job at St Peter's School. Benin City was a very large concentration of human habitation. Being small children it was difficult for us to visualise, especially when we were told that people were always moving about in the streets at all hours of day and night. Apparently there were so many streets that people, especially children, could get lost easily if they lost their bearings. In later years, my sisters Mercy (older than Edward) and Florence and Mabel (both younger than I) completed their primary school education there, at the CMS Girls School located along Sapele Road. By that time I had visited Benin City and it no longer seemed strange. When I went to Benin City for the first time in December 1940, it had three CMS churches – St James's, St Peter's and St Matthew's. St James's Church was popularly referred to as the Foreigners Church in Benin City; the foreigners in question being Nigerians of non-Bini origin. They came from other tribes such as Yoruba, Ibo, Urhobo, Ijaw, Isoko, Itsekiri and Efik, and so on. Worship at St James's Church took place in English with no translation. In contrast worship at St Peter's Church was entirely in Bini language, while at St Matthew's Church worship was in Bini language interspersed with English. The supervising and coordinating priest for these three churches was Reverend Payne who with his wife (both English) resided at the vicarage of St Peter's Church. A primary school was established close by each of these CMS churches.

Penny Penny (Nursery) School

At some time in the 1930's, Reverend and Mrs Payne invited my sister Comfort to help them establish a nursery school at St Peter's School, a new concept in that part of the world and perhaps all of Nigeria. It was a school for toddlers aged between two and five years; the children were brought to school by their parents at 8am and collected by 12 noon; parents were allowed and perhaps encouraged to bring along some snacks and drinks for their children. The fee charged was one penny per week and so the school acquired the Bini title of "Eh Sukul ee kor bee kor bor", an anglicised pronunciation of the Bini expression that meant "The penny penny school". The school caused great excitement initially as many parents wondered what toddlers could learn at school, apart from play and play and play; however, they very quickly appreciated that it gave them the freedom from child minding for about four hours and the opportunity to do essential household chores or go to market. The parents also gradually began to admire how these children built up confidence in themselves in expressing their minds, interacting with other children without shyness, and talking more freely at home to family members as well as to visitors. Whatever these children learnt at school, they promptly came home and endeavoured to teach or practise on their parents, siblings and any other people in the household. Moreover, many of these very young children looked forward to the day when they would be accepted (or perhaps promoted) to the mainstream school, in Kindergarten class one; this opportunity brought a great relief to many parents who would otherwise have faced the difficulty of getting their children into school at age 5 or 6 years.

The structure of education was basically the kindergarten classes 1 and 2 (or Infant classes) for ages 3 to 5 years, lasting two years, followed by Primary Classes 1 to 6. Promotion from one Primary class to the next was usually by success in the end of year examination and the school year was from January to December. Tuition in Primary class 1 was in the local language in the first few months (just as it was in the kindergarten classes) and then the gradual introduction of the English language so that by December, it was totally in English. Primary classes 1 to 6 were sometimes referred to as Standard 1 to 6. However, in the Akoko-Edo District of Benin Province, Yoruba was widely spoken as a second language, in addition to the mother tongue which varied from village to village, or from town to town; hence tuition in Primary 1 was often in Yoruba until changed to English later, in all of Kukuruku district. Consequently, many of the teachers employed by the CMS authorities for schools in Akoko-Edo district were Yoruba indigenes from Oyo, Ondo, Abeokuta, Ijebu and Ekiti tribes. The added advantage of these Yoruba speaking teachers was that they were fully trained teachers from Teacher Training Colleges as compared with the indigenous 'untrained' teachers, who were recruited with only a standard six First School Leaving Certificate.

In Kukuruku district in the thirties, all the mission schools progressed from the kindergarten stage to the primary classes 1 and 2, paused for a year or two, and then when finances improved and facilities and appropriate staff could be provided, were developed to classes 3 and 4.

Empire Day Celebrations

A record of Primary School education in the colonial days would not be complete without recalling Empire Day celebrations. Throughout the school year, games and exercise were organised including running, jumping, sack-races, and egg & spoon races (the latter for girls only). The climax of every school year was the 24th of May, **EMPIRE DAY,** held to celebrate the official birthday of Queen Victoria of England, even though many decades had passed since the Great White Queen had died. As many schools of the district as could organise it, sent contingents of school children to Auchi, the District Headquarters, to take part in these games. The winners of the various events went home with exciting prizes. I recall these as being balloons in different colours, lead pencils with inscriptions, crayons, erasers, exercise books of differing sizes, and even (in later years), white vests (usually called singlets in Nigeria) with or without inscriptions.

Some of the schools were located as far away from Auchi as 20 to 25 miles and I do not remember if and what the respective School Headmasters arranged for their pupils concerning food and drink (water), but at the end of the games, one good meal of boiled rice with meat and stew was served to all participants. Transportation by cars, buses and lorries was not available in those days; everyone walked or trekked using the common parlance. Whenever the group of teachers and pupils in uniform passed through a village on their way, the drummers would beat their drums, the pipers would play a marching tune and the pupils would sing lustily, even though it was obvious that many were exhausted. Any pupil who attracted the attention of the teachers by appearing to be tired and unwilling to sing, would have earned a few strokes of the cane on return to school. The common marching songs taught us in those days by the teachers were colonial songs from Britain and America like Blue Bells of Scotland, Rule Britannia, Marching through Georgia, and, strangely enough, the French National Anthem sung in English. As I recall, it took about another decade or two for local songs and tunes to be accepted as marching songs for use in schools. The colonial influence was very strong in those days, and people were very proud to show that they had acquired colonial 'education'. Not surprisingly, when radio was introduced in the late 1930s to early 1940s, via Rediffusion Boxes, these were boxes that relayed only BBC programmes. I have no doubt this served the government well, especially as the 2nd World War was going on, to ensure that the world news available to the generality of the population had a British flavour and highlighted the gains and advances of British and Allied troops. I was small then, though educationally advanced compared to my classmates, and my parents did not think I could undertake and survive the trek, drill and competitive games at Auchi (24 miles from Otuo) for the Empire Day Celebrations. My recollections recorded here are based on what my older siblings and seniors told me.

The Music Maker

Our new Headmaster in 1937 was Adetunji, a product of St Andrew's College, Oyo. He loved to sing and had learnt to play the harmonium which was a reed organ with foot pedals, during his training. It was therefore not surprising that a slot was provided in the weekly time-table of the school for singing lessons just before school closed on Fridays. It was attended by all the pupils in Primary classes 1 to 4. I recall that in one of these singing classes, he taught us a particular song in pidgin-English; on Monday at the end of the morning assembly, the headmaster invited any pupil who could remember the song taught on the previous Friday to step forward to sing it. He started with the most senior class, Primary 4, then Primary 3, then Primary 2 (my class) and finally Primary 1. I was the only one who was able to sing it all the way through without any mistakes. Headmaster Adetunji then called me to receive an award. I declined at first probably out of shyness, but he insisted and my brother and some other pupils encouraged me to accept the award and I did. It was a coin and I happily put it in my pocket. When school was over and I returned home and told my parents about the singing and the prize and showed them the coin, Baba and Mama rejoiced with me and congratulated me; it was a toro (*pronounced 'taw-raw'*), and I requested Mama to keep it for me. Later, perhaps a few days or even a week, some older boys told me that my prize money was three pence, about half a day's income of an unskilled worker. (By comparison, the income of a 'pupil teacher' (someone employed as a teacher with no training other than his or her Standard 6 certificate) was ten shillings and sixpence a month if a female, and twelve shillings and sixpence a month if a male). That made me even happier than on the day I got the prize.

Adetunji's love of music also made a landmark in the history of the church. When Baba and the church administrative council had decided on the date for the adult Harvest Thanksgiving Celebration, our headmaster sent two mature pupils from Otuo to Okpe, with a letter to the Headmaster and the Catechist there, requesting to be allowed to use the harmonium of the church in Okpe; the Catechist and the Headmaster granted the request and the two 'boys' returned, bringing the harmonium to Otuo. Adetunji was absolutely delighted. Come Sunday, one day later, at the Harvest Thanksgiving Service, the school pupils sang lustily the various songs they had practised for weeks, accompanied by organ music. Baba, Mama, Adetunji and all the teachers and school pupils as well as the entire congregation expressed joy and profound happiness at the service of harvest, and it was the talk of the town of Otuo for many months.

The sound of organ music was not strange to me, my family and visitors in the Mission Compound because Baba had acquired a gramophone some years earlier when we were at Uzairue. He had some 12-inch records which played church music like hymns, canticles and anthems. My brother Edward and I, and my nephew Albert got into trouble in 1934 or 1935 when we quietly went and opened the gramophone, could not operate it, and worse still could not shut it to cover our escapade; I believe we received some well-deserved strokes of the "cane in the corner" of the 'parlour' (the sitting room) and we never tried it again.

Not minding our experience with the gramophone years before, Edward, Albert and I, went back into the church about an hour after the end of the harvest service at Otuo, to acquaint ourselves better with the harmonium; fortunately for us, the Headmaster was still playing the 'organ' and then paused to show us how it worked, the pedals that pumped the bellows that blew air across the reeds that produced the sounds that everyone loved. While we were still there, the harmonium was folded up into a neat rectangular box to await its return to Okpe the following day. This experience fired our imagination and we aspired, in fact resolved to learn to play music and possibly even pipe organs.

All three of us succeeded to varying degrees in the years that followed when we entered post-primary educational institutions. Later Edward acquired a harmonium and still has one, (probably not the earlier one) and two of his children are church organists. I bought a mouth organ which I still have, learned to play the piano in secondary school, acquired a second-hand piano which I later sold and then bought a keyboard, one of the early models which I still have; one of my children played a recorder at school, the sound of which reminded me of the flutes we used when celebrating "Queen Victoria in Nigeria" in years gone by. Albert's love of music was displayed in the acquisition of a large collection of gramophone records of the great masters like Beethoven, Handel, Mozart, Tschaikowsky and others, and the stereo equipment to play them. This included an amplifier, mixer, woofers and tweeters, all in order to produce a high quality sound. We all loved music, a trait that was passed on to us by Baba and Mama and which we in turn passed on to succeeding generations and descendants.

The Little Black Box

Long before I was born, photographers like Alabi had travelled through our districts peddling their trade from one town or village to another. The contraption they used was invariably mounted on a tripod, with a collapsible portion behind the lens through which the photographer looked while his head and the camera were covered with a black piece of cloth. Sometimes the photographer, in order to influence the light of the environment before taking photos, held out another gadget which at the appropriate time exploded and gave out a very bright light for a few seconds. This was all familiar.

In 1936 when my father and our family moved to Otuo on transfer, one of our teachers, Momodu took and passed the examination to gain admission to St Andrews College, Oyo the following year, so as to become a fully trained and certificated teacher after a four-year course of study.[6] In December of the year 1937, during the end of year vacation, he visited us in Otuo and showed us a small black box called a box camera, telling us that it functioned as perfectly as the old gadget that we used to see, if not better, being handy and portable. I was puzzled, flabbergasted and almost unbelieving that that small black box would do what our friend Alabi ('Two times war no good') did with all the paraphernalia with which he toured the district to earn a living.

The day after his arrival, Momodu who was from the royal household of Agbede not far from Auchi, as if reading my mind as to whether his black box could do all he claimed, requested my father to allow him take a family photograph. Baba accepted the offer. As it was the Christmas season, all my brothers and sisters were at home. The family photograph taken included my parents, all my brothers and sisters and myself, as well as some other relatives (nephew, cousins) living with us. Our teacher-friend went home for the rest of his vacation and then returned to Oyo. I waited in suspense and anxiety for what seemed a long, long period. It might have been a week or two or even a month or more that I quietly endured my doubt about the box camera. Then one day, just like any other day, the post was delivered to my father as usual – letters, local and from overseas, magazines and Christian journals from Lagos and overseas, different sizes, some flat and one or two (journals) rolled up. As usual Baba opened the journals first, glanced at them to familiarise himself with what was happening in the Christian world from the viewpoint of the CMS in London. Then he opened the letters. Usually, Baba would have gone on to call my mother to share with her any news, or important information and other developments contained in the mails, and then later, if necessary, he would call us to tell us anything new we needed to know.

Instead, Baba called as usual, "who is there?". One of us answered by name and Baba said "Call everyone to come now". My big sister Mama Benin had returned to Benin City, my two big brothers Alfred and Henry had resumed school at Igarra, leaving my sister Mercy, my brother Edward, myself, my younger sister Florence, my nephew Albert, our baby sister Mabel, cousin James and a few other cousins who were with us, to respond to Baba's call. With great delight, Baba showed us the photo print, postcard size, of the family photograph Momodu had taken in December. [7] It was now January 1938. I looked, and looked, and looked at the postcard size picture; yes it was truly our family photograph, and I recognised everyone in it, especially myself and the dress I wore on that occasion. "So that little black box called a box camera does work as well as Alabi's gadget!" I said to myself.

Three years later in January 1941, I commenced secondary education in Government College, Ibadan. During the first term, every new student had to indicate what hobbies he was interested in, choose three, and then register as a member of the relevant society. The three hobbies I chose were music (playing the piano), boxing and, as can well be predicted, photography. I gave up boxing after about three months because in one practice session, I received a hard punch which caused my nose to bleed. Music, I enjoyed very much, and I made rapid progress with the "Smallwood Pianoforte Tutor" book supervised by our Mathematics Teacher, a brilliant pianist, and an Irishman, Laidlaw was his name. By my third year in Government College, I was quite comfortable playing classics like Beethoven, Mozart and others, from the beginner to the advanced compositions. Photography was a hobby that really fascinated me; the supervising Teacher was Awosika, another mathematics teacher but also an expert and an enthusiastic photographer. I learned the basic principles of taking pictures quite rapidly, using a box camera. I used the darkroom to develop my films and print the photographs, a hobby I enjoyed thoroughly. It was therefore not surprising that at the earliest opportunity, I did not hesitate to spend most of the pocket money that should have covered two school terms in purchasing a box camera. It was a second-hand camera, bought from another student in the society whose taste had matured and advanced from box to folding cameras. As soon as I got the camera, I bought a roll of Kodak film, took some pictures (there were eight exposures in a roll of film), went into the dark room and developed the film, and put it up to dry. The next day after evening meals but before the compulsory study period, I went into the darkroom again and with the help of a classmate friend, printed the photographs, and hung them from a string overhead to dry, overnight. The next day, between our wake-up call and the bell for sports, I dashed into the darkroom to collect my photographs…. joy and satisfaction galore!

Then came our long vacation of six weeks between July and early September, and I went home for the holidays. In my delight and with great enthusiasm, I showed Baba, Mama, and everyone at home the photographs I had taken, developed and printed, all by myself; then I took out my "black box" which was my very own camera, and displayed it expecting the admiration of everyone. Alas! Baba was not impressed at all, *"So you had too much pocket money and you wasted it all buying a camera"* he said, and he gave me a good telling off; I feared that I was going to have a sound treatment from the long cane leaning against the wall at the corner of the sitting room when the divine providence of God saved me. My nephew Albert, two months younger than I, thought the scene was so amusing, that he laughed aloud. Baba turned his attention from me to Albert and reprimanded him. Then Baba said, *"I suppose that when your time comes, you will buy a cinema so as to do better than Felix"*. What Baba really meant was a cine-camera, and sure enough, a few years later, Albert acquired one.

I loved the art of photography. I enjoyed taking snapshots of stills as well as moving objects, working in the darkroom developing and printing them, sometimes even enlarging the prints. Then came colour photography, first the 'sepia' which gave a brown tint to the entire black & white picture, almost like a photograph that had become faded over a number of years; the next development was artificial 'colouring' by the professional photographer in his studio. For true colour pictures in those days, a colour film was inserted in the camera and we would post the exposed film to Kodak in London where it was developed, printed and then posted back. Technology moved rapidly and the 'Polaroid Camera' came into fashion, in the sixties in Nigeria. This enabled us to take a photo, and then develop it without a dark room and print it with all the colours in just a matter of a few minutes.

As the years rolled by, I acquired more sophisticated kit, folding cameras, reflex cameras and detachable lenses, wide angle and zoom and a slide projector. Just about two decades after my initial box camera experience, I acquired a cine camera in time to record the highlights of the Independence Day Celebrations of Nigeria, at the Race Course in Lagos, October 1, 1960 and a Eumig Projector for home films. Subsequently, my parents even allowed me to record some scenes of them at home in Ora.

A few decades later the technological advancement that hit the telephone industry resulted in the smartphone. Anybody from about the age of three years without learning to read or write, could indulge in photography to his or her heart's content, taking pictures or making videos films or even movies. It took about five decades for my elation and sense of achievement regarding photography to pale into insignificance! Forgotten days! I hoped that my cameras and photographic equipment would one day become a decent collection for a museum, but alas, a home-help at some time in the past decade, decided to dispossess me of most of them.

Kukuruku Central School Garra (KCSG)

As time went on and the CMS had more financial resources, they were able to add classes for older pupils to their primary schools until most of them reached Standard 4; In Kukuruku District many mission schools remained at this level for many years. Progression through the classes was by examination only. The government had a school at Auchi that went up to standard 6 and pupils in this class were required to sit an examination for **The First School Leaving Certificate** indicating that they had completed their primary education. But pupils in the mission schools who attained Standard 4 could only hope to complete their primary education by relocating to other districts and even cities far away.

When Baba was transferred from Uzairue to Otuo in early

1936 I moved to the mission school, St Stephen's CMS School in Otuo. It went up to Standard 4, and was well established. I started in Standard 1 but with the advantage of having several older siblings and overhearing them do their homework many evenings, I had already picked up a lot of knowledge. Consequently, I spent just six months in Standard 2 and with a good overall assessment, was moved to Standard 3 for the remaining six months of the year. With more specific help from my brother Edward, I was able to obtain a good result in the end of year examinations and moved on to Standard 4. It was now 1938. Two of my older brothers, Alfred and Henry, had been 'going away' during the week and returning home at weekends. They had passed out of Standard 4 two years earlier, and needed to leave Otuo in order to complete their primary education in a school that went up to Standard 6. They came home on Friday evenings at dusk, and left again on Sunday afternoon, packing as many food items as they could manage to carry. Baba also gave them some pocket money, how much I did not know; what I did gather over time was that in their school they had to provide for and cook their own meals, and that all the children, boys and girls, in that school resided in the school premises. The boys stayed in dormitories, and the girls resided in the home of the Catechist of the adjacent CMS Church. I had heard of boarding schools for secondary age children in far off towns and cities, but I was puzzled to learn that it applied to Primary School education. And I and other members of the household were always keen for the two older brothers to tell us what it was like. I was fascinated.

Their school was called Kukuruku Central School, Garra (KCSG) and had been established by the CMS in 1936 to provide one school with Standards 5 and 6 to meet the educational aspirations of mission school pupils in the entire District. Admission was by entrance examination, and only the best of the successful candidates were selected. With an intake of about thirty pupils, the school year started in January immediately after the

Christmas holidays. Colonial Administrative Authorities called the town Garra but today it is called Igarra as known in the indigenous language.

Come mid-January 1939, it was time for a radical change in my school life pattern. I had passed the examination held in December 1938, with a good score and was offered admission to KCSG; so also was my brother Edward, as well as James, a little older than my brother, and an Auchi indigene who lived with my father at the request of his father. It was a blessing from God that all three of us were admitted to Standard 5 at KCSG, at the same time. As can be imagined, I helped with sweeping and tidying part of the dormitory as required while Edward and James did the cooking, fetching water from the river and firewood from the bush.

Igarra, if I may now use the appropriate name, is in a pocket of the savannah region of Nigeria, with few spindly scattered trees and a lot of tall grasses. Drinking water was fetched from a stream running from the rocky hillside, clean at all times, about half an hour walking distance from the school while water for washing was fetched from a river another 10-15 minutes further away, and nearer Igarra Oke. Sketch 2

KCSG was located on a plateau uphill from Igarra Sale (pronounced sah-ler, meaning 'lower level'), while Igarra Oke (pronounced oh-kay, meaning upper level) was located about a mile to a mile and half on a downward slope along the road to Auchi. I was puzzled for some weeks that Igarra Oke seemed to be at a lower level than Igarra Sale, but later I reflected that the names 'Oke' and 'Isale' (up and down) indicated the pre-colonial locations of those towns on the hills before their people migrated to the plains, where their position became reversed.

I believe I was easily the youngest and smallest pupil in the school but what astonished me was that some pupils, a few in my class, and more in Standard 6, were married and had children; they were generally not among the brightest academically, and hence barely tolerated arguments with us the younger ones. They often tried to silence us as little children, inexperienced in worldly affairs, and who should be seen and not heard. From time to time we the younger ones encouraged them by asking them to tell us about married life and how they blended it with still going to school; a few of them more reserved by nature, would say 'just wait until your time comes, you'll find out'. Those who were more outgoing and obviously delighted to have an audience to boost their ego, eagerly fed us with details of their life styles and responsibilities, including sometimes details of their intimate relations; they would then suddenly, after satisfying their younger audience with fairy-tale-like fantasies, say **"oh, you are too young to understand all this"** and then they would dry up.

There were two classes, each with about 25 pupils, boys and girls, and there were two dormitories (for boys only), while the girls resided with the Catechist just a few minutes' walk away.[sketch 3] There was only one girl in my class, Comfort Ohiorhenuan, from a family well known to us, on my father's side, quite a brilliant girl and about the same age as my brother Edward. Her father was the Catechist that Baba had relieved at Uzairue only a few years earlier.

The daily routine was simple. The day started with a wake-up bell by the Prefect in the dormitory at 6am; all the pupils hurried and got up from their sleeping mats, rolled them up and put them away. Some had their baths while others immediately prepared their breakfast; it was quite common to have pounded yam for breakfast, and there being only one set of mortar and pestle in each dormitory, pupils shouted one after the other the order in which they would pound their yams, and the system was conscientiously adopted and adhered to; other pupils ate beans cooked the previous evening, boiled yam, or eba (gari in boiled water) served with soup previously cooked.

School began with morning assembly and prayers by 8am, and went on till 2pm, with a break in the mid-morning. After class was over, there was lunch according to the individual pupils' taste, a little rest, and then the afternoon programme of sports, usually football or athletics. Rather strange but I do not now remember if there was any scheduled programme for the night. We ate, studied or did any homework assigned by the teacher and then went to sleep by 9.30pm when all lights had to be put out.

The Headmaster in 1939 when I entered KCSG was Fakoya, a product of St Andrew's College, an Ijebu man who was married, and loved music. Hence there was a well scheduled provision in the school curriculum for 'singing' and, most of the time, he taught us church music, hymns, anthems and choruses. Because of this, churches in the District often invited us to sing at their annual Harvest Thanksgiving or other special services and we were considered to be *"fantastic, an asset to be experienced, to fully appreciate wonderful singing"*. One of the songs frequently rendered was "Ye holy angels bright, who wait at God's right hand". We sang in English or Yoruba as requested by the host Church, but more often in Yoruba than in English.

Singing was good and I loved singing from my younger days, but what I remember most vividly about these excursions to distant village churches was not the singing, nor the rather tedious walking to some of them about five or six miles from Igarra. Rather, it was the opportunity it gave us to wear our "school blazers": navy blue coats with white stripes and KCSG embroidered on a patch over the breast pocket. These coats had been donated by the C.M.S. authorities in Lagos. They were in different sizes and the pupils selected the size that best fitted them before setting out on each excursion. They belonged to and remained the property of the School, so that pupils used them for two years and left them behind upon leaving the school. The wonderful thing about it all was that KCSG pupils arrived in church in style and departed again in style, singing in a manner that the host churches remembered for a long time. By the grace of God Almighty, in all these trips to sing in churches away from Igarra, we were not caught or beaten by rain, which would have made things rather awkward.

Pupils and Domestic service

It was not uncommon in those days for headmasters or teachers to arrange for some pupils whose homes were far away to reside with the headmaster or a teacher to provide domestic service such as sweeping the house, washing and ironing clothes, as well as cooking for male teaching staff who were unmarried. In return, the headmaster or teacher paid the pupil's school fees and was responsible for their upkeep and maintenance. Our headmaster in 1939, Fakoya, had two pupils residing with him. One was Nathaniel Odubola Oduyemi, a relation, and the other was Jeremiah Olatunji from Imeri; both were in standard 6. Many years later, I met Odubola when I was a doctor at Igbobi Hospital; he had established himself as a printer and had a printing press. As for Olatunji, he became a teacher before branching off into party politics and became very active in what was then known as the Mid-West Region of Nigeria taking the name Chief J O Oye, abbreviated from his original surname of Amoboye.

Whether it was sheer coincidence or whether the policy was engineered because of the war I do not know, but in Sept/Oct 1939, the government of Nigeria decided to modify the education system for the country. The First School Leaving Certificate Examination at the end of Standard Six was centrally organised from Lagos and so the certificate issued was subsequently headed *'First School Leaving Certificate'* and in brackets below it *'As amended*

1939', but there was no observable change in the syllabus. Somehow this did not go down very well with many people, and one way of expressing this resentment was that the interest in secondary education grew tremendously, with hopes of acquiring a straight forward certificate without any reservation implied in the expression "As amended 1939". I got swept up by this wave of thinking and feeling and, determined to fulfil my father's hope for my further education, I decided from the beginning of 1940 that I would endeavour to go to secondary school.

One of my classmates at KCSG, Felix Ijomah, became a good friend, and he often talked to me about his older brother Donatus, a student in Government College Ibadan. After some months, I began to correspond with Donatus as a pen-friend. As time went by, I built up a picture in my mind as to what life in Government College Ibadan was like, and I would tell my friend Felix that it would be nice if both of us got accepted into that college for our secondary school education. His focus however was different, he was interested in Edo College Benin City, Dennis Memorial Grammar School, Onitsha, or Christ the King's College Onitsha. At weekends when we went home, I would discuss what I had learnt from Felix Ijomah with my parents. Years later, I came to realise that the name we spelt as Ijomah was an anglicised version of Ijeoma (or Ijeomah) as it would be spelt today.

In the entire Kukuruku District, there was no secondary school; consequently, pupils aspired to enter well known institutions like Edo College Benin City, Government Colleges in Lagos (King's and Queen's), Ibadan and Umuahia, Grammar Schools in Lagos, Abeokuta and Ibadan, St Gregory's College Lagos, Igbobi College Lagos, DMGS and CKC in Onitsha, and Hussey College Warri. There were more secondary schools in other parts of Nigeria at the time but information about them was scarcely available in Kukuruku District.

For girls, secondary education seemed possible only in faraway Lagos, where Queens College and other girls' secondary schools were located. The alternatives were Teacher Training institutions and the most popular of these was the United Missionary College (UMC) Ibadan.

The second teacher at KCSG in 1939, was Oni, an Ekiti indigene, who was trained at St Andrews College. A few months after I entered KCSG, he went for a 9-months training course, to the School of Agriculture, Moor Plantation, Ibadan. On his return in early 1940, he took over as Headmaster from Fakoya who was transferred away from Igarra and the District. The pupils now had the benefit of being taught principles of agriculture in basic farming such as crop rotation, how to use mucuna beans to enrich the soil, and so on.

Because of these staff shortages, short term appointments of teachers became imperative. One such teacher was E F Smith, an Itsekiri man, who spoke softly, and had a gentle nature. He later went to Awka College of Divinity, where he trained to become a Priest in the Anglican church. Later still, he was posted to Benin City as the Pastor in charge of St James' Church, my sister Mama Benin's church. Rev Smith, his wife and children became our close family friends.

Another short-term teacher was G A Alele, from Sobe near Ora; he had been Headmaster of St Stephen's School Otuo when I was a pupil there, and, being married to a relation of my mother, was well known to our family.

A lot more could be written about KCSG, especially how it formed the basis of future academic, social and political advancement and attainment for many individuals, but alas, its life span was brief. After about a decade, it was snuffed out of existence because many schools in the District developed and recruited well-trained teachers to run their own Standards 5 and 6 classes. KCSG had become a historical curiosity in the educational annals of the CMS.

Preparing for post-primary education

My father often called Albert (Mama Benin's son), Edward and me, together to advise us to focus our educational ambition on post-primary education and hopefully to become University graduates. Baba knew about St Andrew's College, Oyo the teacher training college that also offered theological training; and Edo College, Benin City, a secondary school that offered just the first four years only and not the six years required for students to do the Senior Cambridge Examination. With the ongoing Second World War, information available to Baba was that Government College Ibadan might not admit new students in 1941 because of the logistical difficulties of conducting a nation-wide entrance examination.

About three months before the end of 1940, Baba was transferred from Otuo northward to Ikiran Ile, in the Akoko-Edo area of Kukuruku District. The information reached us in school at Igarra that our parents had moved already. So the following weekend, James, Edward and I identified some pupils at KCSG who were going home to Ikiran-Ile and journeyed with them. The route was fascinating in that while there was a motorable road all the way from Igarra to Ikiran-Ile via Aiyegunle and Ibillo, a foot-path from Aiyegunle direct to Ikiran Ile reduced the overall distance by about half, rather like the hypotenuse of a right-angled triangle. The journey on foot lasted about two to two and half hours.

By November ending, Rev. Akinluyi, a cousin of ours, sent a message to Baba telling him a date in the first week of December for the Government College Ibadan entrance examination.

The examination was to take place in Benin City.[5] I knew Baba and Mama must have prayed fervently about this, and the next thing I remember was that my brother Henry came to Igarra by bicycle to ensure quick arrival over the eight-mile journey via the footpath. He had come with a letter from my father requesting the Headmaster to kindly release me to go to Benin City for the entrance examination to Government College Ibadan. The next morning Henry and I set out for Benin, with Henry riding the bicycle, while I sat on the bar, dismounting only for the hills which I climbed on foot. Getting to Auchi, 21 miles from Igarra, we found a lorry that took us and the bicycle part of the way. I cannot recall whether it stopped at Ewu or Irrua but from there we cycled to Ekpoma and rested in the Mission House. The next morning a goods lorry was available, so we left the bicycle in Ekpoma and travelled to Benin City, arriving to the great surprise of my sister, Mama Benin who welcomed us with shouts of joy and prayers, just like Baba and Mama. A few days later, on the appointed day, I was taken to the Office of the Education Department in Benin City in the morning, and I sat the examination together with other children. It was supervised in person, by J.G. Speer, the Education Officer for Benin Province at the time, an English man. At the end of the examination we were told to go home, and that those candidates who performed well would be invited to return to Benin for an interview in January 1941. My brother and sister who had waited patiently for me outside, took me home and the next day Henry and I set out for Auchi by lorry, picking up the bicycle along the way. The final part of the journey was again entirely by cycle to Igarra; school had closed for the December holidays, and Edward and James had gone home, so Henry and I cycled to Ikiran-Ile, via the footpath. The journey to Benin City, the examination, and the return journey home was, in a way, quite an exciting and interesting adventure for me. Baba and Mama were very happy to see us back home safely.

At our daily family devotional prayers, Baba and Mama prayed for my success in the recent examination, in addition to thanking God for the successful completion of our primary education at Igarra. Early in January 1941, the results of the Standard 6 Examination held in December 1940 were released. James, Edward and I had passed and were now qualified to receive our First School Leaving Certificate (as amended in 1939). How wonderful !

All my older siblings went into the teaching profession after completing their primary school education and my brother Edward was also inclined towards a teaching career. James who had become like a family member to us decided to go to Lagos to seek employment; he got a job with The Nigerian Railways where he worked meritoriously until he retired and returned home to Auchi.

Chapter 7

GOVERNMENT COLLEGE IBADAN

About the end of the first week in January 1941 after all the celebrations of eating, drinking and wearing new clothes at Christmas and the New Year, a letter came by post from the Education Department in Benin City. I was invited to Benin City on a named date for an interview for possible admission to GCI having performed well in the examination held in December. And so once again Henry and I made the arduous journey to Benin but this time, without the bicycle. We took the journey in stages by lorry, Ikiran-Ile to Auchi where we stayed overnight with a family friend. Then early the next morning we walked two miles' distance to Jattu Market where there was a big lorry park. We boarded a lorry from there to Benin where we stayed with Mama Benin. On the day scheduled for the interview, I went again to the Education Department Office in Benin City where about half a dozen pupils were waiting. We sat an examination in English and Arithmetic, after which we were interviewed, one by one. By the end of the interviews, the written papers had already been marked, and only two of us, Gabriel Imasuen from Benin City and I, were called back into the office where we were informed that we had been successful and that we would receive our letters of admission by post, confirming the admission date of which we were told there and then. Mama Benin was overjoyed at the good news and we made our way to see Reverend Smith who was delighted and prayed for us and with us. Henry and I made our journey back to Ikiran-Ile and the joy and happiness of Baba and Mama was without bounds. We all rejoiced and prayed joyfully everyday as we prepared for the date when I would travel to Ibadan. Sure enough, the letter arrived by post and Baba opened it cautiously, with great anticipation and then exploded with joy, shouting and telling every one that I had been given a scholarship, too. The prayer bell rang and we prayed and thanked God for His blessings. The scholarship meant that full board and uniforms, books, pens, pencils, erasers etc would be made available, for free. In fact, the only expenses Baba would incur were the transport costs to and from school every term, three times a year. How wonderful! I found out later that fee-paying (non-scholarship) students were required to pay sixteen pounds per annum, well in excess of Baba's entire annual income as a Catechist.

Preparation for my departure went into full swing but there was really very little to prepare because of the scholarship. A modest size wooden box was made to hold the few things I needed to take, that I could conveniently carry on my head even if it was full. From time to time Mama expressed her anxiety that Ibadan was far, far, far from Kukuruku and she would not be able to visit me to see how I was getting on. Baba just smiled and comforted her that all would be well because one could see the hand of God in it all.

Journey to the Unknown

The day for my departure from home came closer and closer and finally arrived. As can well be imagined, my parents could not and did not entertain the possibility of my travelling by myself alone, all the way to Ibadan; I was twelve and a half years old, but had not undertaken any journey alone from home exceeding one mile. As usual, my older brother Henry was assigned to see me safely admitted to college in Ibadan, and we set out with my wooden box. I do not remember what I took. This time we travelled without the bicycle, by passenger lorry as distinct from the goods lorries that carried palm kernels, or cocoa beans in large jute bags; such lorries always seemed to be able to find space to accommodate two, three, or four passengers as long as they had no significant luggage.

We went from Ikiran-Ile to Auchi and then on to Benin City where Mama Benin was overjoyed to see us. She prayed to God, thanking Him that Felix (that's me) was going to be a student of Government College Ibadan, and on scholarship too. We travelled by Armel's Transport overnight direct from Benin City to Ibadan, stopping at quite a few towns including Owo, Akure, Igbara Oke, Ilesha, Ile-Ife, Gbongan and finally Ibadan. At each of these stops, some passengers alighted and others boarded. Sometimes the stop was just to allow the passengers (like Henry and me) to stretch our legs, having been cramped in our seats for hours, to buy and eat food, as well as disappear into the nearby bush to ease ourselves as necessary; there were no public toilets in these smaller towns in those days, unlike Benin City, Ibadan and Lagos which all had public toilets. After an all-night journey we arrived in Ibadan, at dawn, alighted and did our best to brush off the red dust that by now, was uniformly spread over our heads, faces, arms, legs and clothes. Henry enquired of people around who appeared likely to be able to help us and they directed us towards Ogunpa and Oke Bola. Upon getting there, we were to ask for Ijebu By-Pass and we would find the College along that road, a distance of about a mile from Oke Bola. I carried my box and heard Henry telling one or two people "No! No! Oti! Oti!" They had shouted "Aaru, Aaru" indicating that they could carry our luggage (my box) to our destination for a price. We followed the directions given to us, and after walking about 30-40 minutes, located the Ijebu By-pass road from Oke Bola, which we took after confirming from other pedestrians that it was the way to Government College. There were no buses or taxis in those days. As we walked along, we saw ahead of us two people just like us, a man walking beside a small boy about the same size and age as myself who was also carrying a box on his head. As we got closer we found to our surprise that they were speaking our language, Ora to each other! Henry greeted them in Ora, and they responded cheerfully but were also surprised and we soon learned that they were also heading to Government College. That is how I met Theophilus Obadan who was to be my classmate, a lifelong friend and in-law, as he later married my cousin Rosebud Usidame, one of twins. Henry introduced us as brothers, he being a teacher, and they introduced themselves as Theophilus and his older brother Mike, a professional photographer resident in Ibadan.

A Girls' College for Boys

Going through the entrance gate, we were ushered into the Administration Office for registration. I was assigned No.340 and led to Grier House dormitory while Theophilus was No.345 and was led to Swanston House dormitory. These numbers indicated the total number of students admitted since the inception of the College in 1929. There were only two Houses in Government College in those days. Having been received into Grier House by someone who I supposed was a Prefect, I bid Henry goodbye and farewell and he set off on his journey back home.

I felt wonderful especially as I looked around me. I had a bed made from wooden slabs resting on 6-inch high trestles off the floor and a bedside locker all to myself. What a difference from my boarding school days in KCSG. Water was available from taps for drinking and for the showers in the bathrooms and also in the squat flush toilets. There was also a deep well with a lift pump for water if and when supply from the Water Board failed.

I enquired after Donatus Ijomah and introduced myself. He was the elder brother to Felix, my classmate at KCSG and he welcomed me heartily, telling me to let him know if I ever had any problems or difficulties. He was in class 6, his final year, and we remained good friends.

Shortly after my admission, the Head of House, the most senior of all the House Prefects, made it clear to all new students that there were some fundamental issues we had to tackle, and some vital information we must learn and know well. First of all, as a student in Grier House I was now a Grierson, and proud to be so; I would be assigned to a 2nd year student who would teach me the history of the House from the inception of the College in 1929; that as a new student I was expected to address all senior students as "Sir" even including second year students; that all students should be addressed and called by their surnames only; and most importantly, that only English language shall be spoken while the College is in session from the opening assembly at the beginning of term to the closing assembly when the term ended and vacation began. And so it was that I was assigned to Ifaturoti, M.A., as my teacher (his older brother Ifaturoti E.A. was also a Government College student, in his 5th year and also in Grier House). At the end of a month all the new students were tested on the House History, and I passed. I learnt later that if I had failed there would have been a repeat examination a few weeks later and my 'teacher' and I would have had to take that repeat examination together. This was to ensure that the student 'teacher' took his responsibility seriously.

About a week later, I received a letter by post from Baba saying Henry had returned home safely and had reported how he saw me settled into Government College Ibadan. Baba again wished me a happy stay in the college, and God's blessings, reminding me once more that I must pray every day and work hard at my studies and not get carried away with play.

Government College Ibadan (GCI) offered six years of study, the first year being called class 2B, second year as class 2A, and the other classes were known as classes 3, 4, 5 and 6. At the end of six years students took the Senior Cambridge Examination organised by Cambridge University, England and I learnt that most students achieved Grades 1 and 2; therefore Grade 3 was regarded in GCI as poor and a let-down; total failure was virtually unknown and was a disaster. I absorbed all this information with trepidation, hoping that I would be able to maintain the expected standard. Notwithstanding the standard programme, one candidate in Class 5 in 1941 was allowed by the College authorities to register and sit for the Senior Cambridge Examination because he was assessed as brilliant and capable. He did not disappoint the College - the results came out early 1942 and he achieved a Grade I pass. His name was Okuboyejo (formerly Oseni) and he later studied medicine and did very well. The standing practice in GCI was that any class 2B student found at the end of the year to have performed outstandingly well academically, was given a double promotion to Class 3 at the beginning of his 2nd year, entirely at the discretion of the College authorities. Each student's assessment scores including the weekly, bi-weekly, monthly, June and December examination scores were added together to form a significant basis for the consideration of such double promotion. We referred to the system as 'collecting marks'. The more mature students on admission were aware of this system and worked towards taking advantage of it, while the younger students were quite happy to work at their 'normal' pace to do their best at all times.

As at January 1941, Grier House had two dormitories, Arubayi and Odiase; Ifaturoti M.A. had told me that Arubayi was for students in Classes 2B, 2A and 3 while Odiase was for the senior classes 4, 5, and 6 students. It was also at this time I learnt very significant information, that GCI was living in borrowed premises. I was flabbergasted. The College home ground and permanent site was at Apata Ganga (the Yoruba name for Big Rocks) area of Ibadan, just beyond Moor Plantation, the Agricultural Research Establishment about three miles out of Ibadan on the Ibadan-Abeokuta main road. There were actually some massive rocks near the main entrance of the College near the highway, though not

Photo 1: Baba and Mama, my parents page 8

Photo 2: Mama Benin page 34

Photo 3: My eldest brother Alfred and I, many years later [page 24]

Photo 4: my elder brother Henry and I ^{page 17}

Archdeacon (Venerable) S O Akinluyi page 55

Photo 6: Mr Momodu our Agbede teacher at Otuo

My Family 1. Alfred 2. Henry 3. Mercy 4. Grace 5. Baba 6. Mama 7. Mabel (standing) 8. Comfort 9. Edward 10. Felix 11. James 12. Ojehnmo (Mama's nephew) 13. Floremce 14. Albert

Photo 8: My brother Edward and his Bride, Grace Modupe ^{page 109}

Photo 9: My nephew Albert, Comfort's son page 116

Photo 10: Ayo Onifade's wedding (I was best man) page 102

Photo 11: Wedding photo of Claris & Me page 103

Photo 12: Dr Cookey-Gam and medical students
1. George 2. Eruchalu 3. Atunrase 4. Steward 5. Onifade
6. Steward 7. Orhewere 8. Ngu 9. Udeozo
10. Ogbeide 11. Okungbowa 12. Miss Yoloye 13. Dr Cookey-Gam
14. Miss Sodipe 15. Akinla 16. Audu

Photo 14: Some medical students at the hostel after Dr Cookey-Gam wedding
1. Orhewere 2. Eruchalu 3. Onifade 4. George 5. Ngu [page 83]

Photo 15: UCI Foundation Laying Ceremony, Sir Arthur Creech Jones and Dr Kenneth Mellamby page 81

Photo 16: UCI Inauguration Day Academic Procession page 81

Photo 17, Ex GCI students at UCI inauguration in 1948
1. Orhewere
2. Akande
3. Onifade
4. Ogunsina
5. Ngu

Photo 18: Dr Hendry, Lecturer in Biochemistry and twelve medical students
1. Akinla 2. Okungbowa 3. Onifade 4. Ngu 5. George 6. Orhewere
7. Eruchalu 8. Audu 9. Ogbeide 10. Miss Sodipe 11. Dr Hendry 12. Udeozo
13. Nwabuoko

Photo 19: Claris and Christie 1952 page 103

Photo 20: Christening of our son Michael page 96

Photo 21: Guys Hospital, *above*: class of 51-52 *below*: class of 61

Photo 22: Claris and I in Benin City page 122

Claris in Gwagwalada

Photo 23: Registered post between 1948 and 1950 page 85

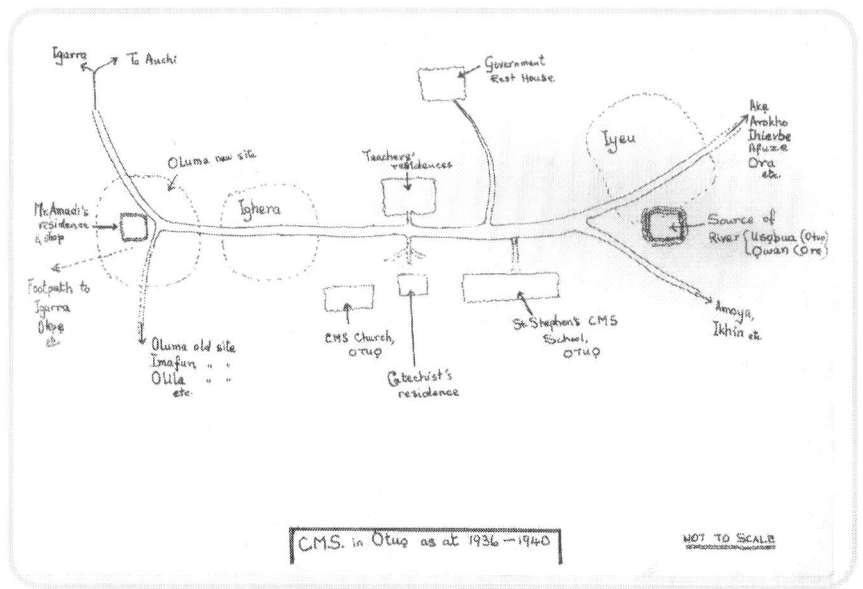

Sketch 1: Otuo 1936 - 1940 page 29

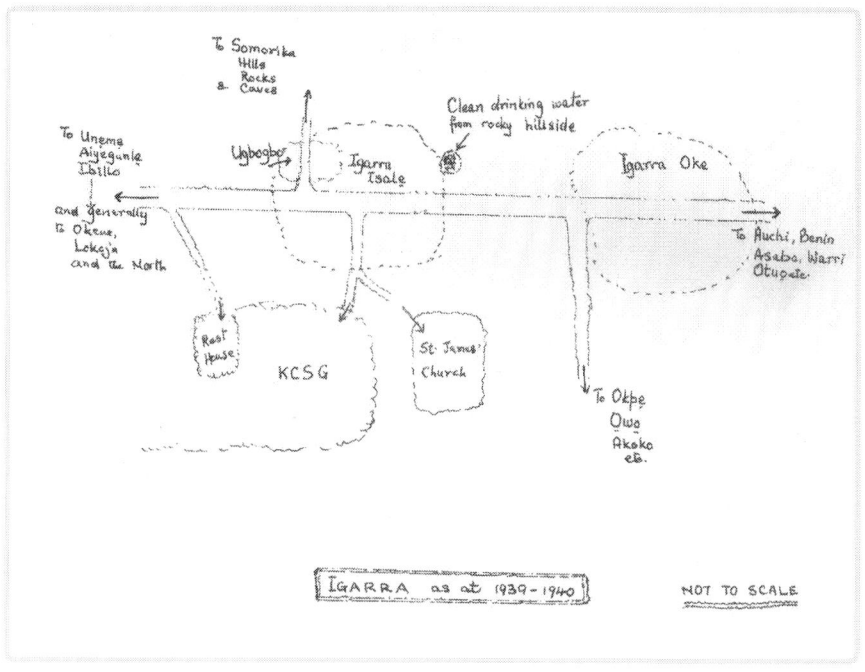

Sketch 2: 1939 to 1940 Igarra 1939 -1940 page 48

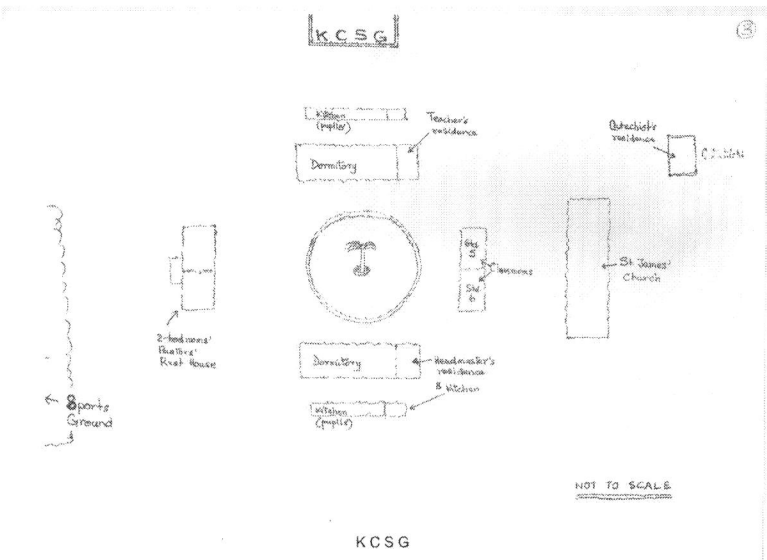

Sketch 3: KCSG page 48

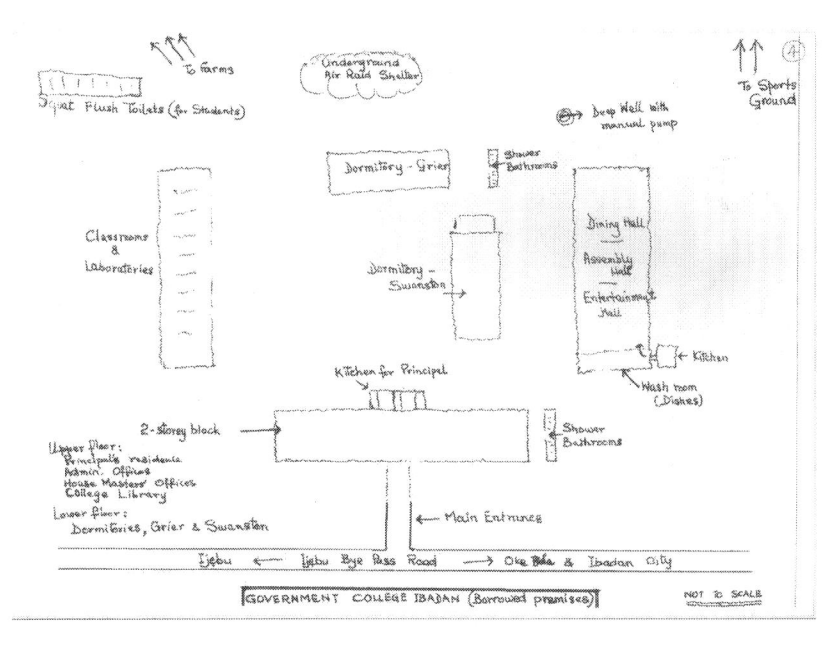

Sketch 4: GCI - Temporary Site, 1944 to 1946 page 63

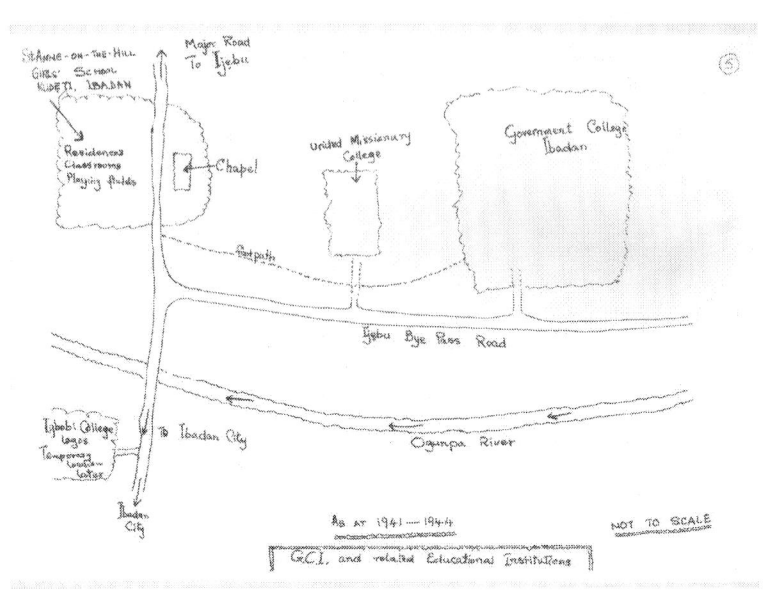

Sketch 5: UMC, St Anne and Igbobi College page 67

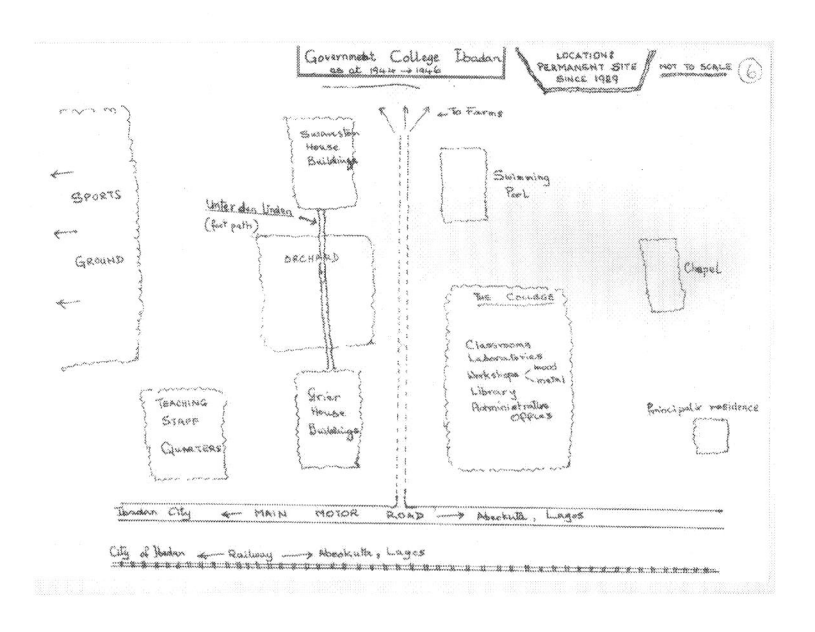

Sketch 6: GCI - Permanent site page 70

large enough to be reckoned as a tourist attraction. When I entered Government College in January 1941 we were in the newly built premises of St Theresa College for Girls, of the Roman Catholic Mission, which I believe was still located in Lagos. Because of the on-going Second World War, Government College had been ordered by the Colonial Administration to vacate its permanent site so that it could be used to accommodate German nationals from different parts of Nigeria and the Cameroons, in political detention until a decision could be taken about their future. The college was fortunate in being able to relocate to this site on the Ijebu Bye Pass.^{Sketch 4}

It was a beautiful location and all the buildings but one were of solid concrete. That one, my Arubayi dormitory, was a partly wooden structure such as was often seen in military barracks and was probably constructed just before the relocation of GCI. Further away from the main road and well beyond the buildings was an Air Raid Underground Shelter. Still further away up the hill on a level piece of ground a vast sports ground was built during my studentship, for athletics, football and cricket. All the students were involved in the grading, levelling and planting of Bahama grass on this new sports field. This was a type of grass that required regular watering for a period after which it survived through all seasons. Without doubt, the students and also the staff very much enjoyed using the facilities we had worked on and established. Government College in those days, was in the forefront of promoting sports activities in Nigeria, and perhaps the best known activity was the Grier Cup Competition in athletics for all interested secondary schools throughout Nigeria. Football and cricket matches were also held on our sports ground. In those days, the printing of advertising posters was not available in Nigeria (or perhaps very, very expensive and beyond the financial reach of our College) and for most of those events, our College Arts Teacher, Ibrahim, drew and hand painted all the posters. They were displayed all over

Ibadan. I do remember that all the events were well attended by the public from Ibadan and beyond. Students cut palm fronds from the surrounding bush to build a shade over the chairs and benches for paying spectators while the rest of the space round the field was used by standing spectators, all free and no cover. For convenience, and taking the climate and weather into consideration, the sporting activities were rotated seasonally in the school terms, with athletics from January to March, football from April to July and cricket from September to December. Swimming took place all year round when the college moved back to its permanent site at Apata Ganga but was suspended while we were at Ijebu Bye Pass.

Angelic Voices

Singing was a subject in the school curriculum in all the primary schools in those days and it usually took place on Fridays for the pupils in Standards 1-6. Infant pupils had their singing classes more frequently each week, virtually every day, as the singing of English nursery rhymes as well as local songs in Yoruba was cherished by every school pupil, something that non-school going children envied. Come to think of it now, that may have been the silent attraction for children to go to register in school, a desire that many parents could not well persist in refusing their children, even though they did not experience it themselves during their childhood.

When I went to Benin City to take the entrance examination for admission to GCI, it was the time of end-of-year school activities, and I got the opportunity to attend an annual social occasion in Benin. Each year, the pupils of CMS Girls School, Benin City, put on nativity plays woven around the birth of Jesus as recorded in the Bible, and sang songs from local folklore as well as Christian songs. The English headmistress, assisted by two or three other English teachers did a marvellous job in bringing out the singing and acting talent in the girls to thrill the audience, while the Nigerian teachers were visibly active in stage management and prompting, as well as ushering members of the audience, on arrival, to their seats. I was greatly impressed by the singing and the performances. Women in the audience were neatly arrayed in European-style dresses or skirts and blouses and some wore hats. The men wore white suits (coat and trousers), white helmets or light coloured trilby hats, and arrived riding well cleaned bicycles. I formed the impression that every 'who is who' in Benin City except the monarch, was present at the CMS Girls' School end-of-year programme. After I returned home to Ikiran-Ile and for the next few weeks, the singing in Benin kept coming to my memory from time to time. I thought it sounded fantastic. The following month I went to Ibadan where the beautiful singing in another girls' school was to leave a memorable impression on me.

Life in the College

The uniform worn to school daily was white shirt with khaki (light brown) shorts and on Sundays we wore white shirts with white shorts, all made of plain drill cotton; no student was allowed to wear clothes made of a different fabric, irrespective of the student's financial or social background. Significantly, these shorts had no side pockets but only right hip pockets. The students believed the style was to discourage a bad habit of many young men in those days of walking around with their hands in their pockets. By the time I became a senior student in 1944 (Class 4), the school regulation was amended so that senior students (classes 4,5 and 6) wore white long trousers with conventional side pockets instead of shorts, on Sundays.

Our religious life in GCI was organised as follows:

1) Every student took part in the Morning Assembly in which a hymn was sung from the original 'Hymns Ancient and Modern' (there were more than enough copies for every

teacher and student to have one each), and prayers were said by the Principal or a Senior Teacher. Announcements followed and finally, there was the attendance roll call by the Head of School. He was the Senior Prefect chosen by the Principal from the Class 6 students, and usually, it was the student who scored the highest marks at the promotion examination in the preceding December.

2)   All the recognised Muslim students had a visiting Imam on Friday mornings who for about 45 minutes delivered Islamic religious instruction, and conducted Islamic prayers.

3)   Roman Catholics students were allowed out on Sunday mornings under the supervision of a senior student, to attend early morning mass in the nearest Catholic Church in town, and these students were served fish on Fridays while all other students had beef.

4)   On Sunday mornings, all students except Muslims and Catholics, went to the girls' school, St Anne on the Hill CMS Girls' School, Kudeti, Ibadan, a walking distance of about a mile and half from GCI using a bush path.

5)   All students without exception attended the Term Opening Assembly at 6.00pm on day of return from the holidays, and the End of Term Assembly on vacation day, at about 9 a.m.

On the social level, there was practically no interaction between the boys of Government College and the girls of Kudeti, presumably because the girls were much younger. That apparent or seeming social void was filled to a great extent by the College authorities in arranging social interaction with the students of United Missionary College, popularly known as U.M.C., a Teacher Training College for girls, located about midway on the footpath from GCI to St Anne's School. The United Missionary College offered a three-year teacher training programme for post-Primary girls, who were admitted after an entrance examination and interview. As the name implies, the college was established as a joint venture by different Missions, to train teachers for their various primary and post-primary educational institutions across the entire country. Sketch 5

When I started at Government College we did not have much interaction with other schools except in sports. Ibadan Grammar School interacted with us in football and athletics. But two to three years later, Igbobi College based in Lagos Island, moved to Ibadan temporarily while their new permanent home was being built on Lagos Mainland at Igbobi, Yaba. This gave us the opportunity to interact with them socially and in debates, in addition to the annual athletics, football and cricket events that had existed between the two colleges for years. St Theresa College also came from Lagos to sojourn in Ibadan on a temporary site until we could vacate and return their premises to them.

World at War

In my first year at Government College a Class 4 student Olopade, who was good at writing in shorthand which he had learnt before coming to the College was given facilities to listen to the Principal's radio every morning, so as to transcribe the 7am BBC World News. This transcription was read to the Assembly every morning after prayers, announcements, and roll call. As can readily be imagined given that the Second World War was ongoing, most of the news was about the war, especially how the British forces and later the Allied British, American and Russian Forces fared. The losses were reported in brief while the advances were always reported in greater detail.

Another war-time feature of school life was the Air Raid Underground Shelter (or Bunker). Drills took place at intervals that were unannounced to the student body. The drill began at the sound of a siren, blowing of whistles, and ringing of a handbell. This was the alert used for an air raid. We were expected to proceed quickly without stampeding into the underground shelter, where we would remain until the "all-clear" siren sounded, and then return to our dormitories. The drill was usually carried out at night, although we were instructed clearly that the same procedure was to be followed if the alert sounded in the day time, even if it sounded during class sessions. It was imperative that any organised programme must be stopped and the procedure to move to the air raid shelter strictly adhered to. Fortunately there was no raid by German aircraft over Ibadan throughout the war, but we did hear news of a bombing raid in Lagos when I was in Class 2 and also that a German U-boat (submarine) was sighted in Lagos Harbour.

Divine Control

In mid-January 1943 just about the end of the Christmas vacation for all schools, primary as well as secondary, I was due to return to GCI. My nephew Albert, having passed the entrance examination held in 1942 to Edo College Benin City, was due to resume there. My parents arranged with Mama Benin that my younger sister Florence should go with her to complete her primary education in Benin City. As a consequence of the on-going Second World War, motor vehicle public transportation had become irregular due to government rationing of petrol. When Baba was told that there was a lorry due to leave or pass through Ikiran Ile to go to Owo, he promptly arranged for Mama Benin, Albert, Florence and myself to travel by it, in the hope that there would be no difficulty finding transport from Owo to Benin, part of the major highway from Lagos to Eastern Nigeria. We arrived at Owo about 7.30 to 8.00pm, and on enquiry about transports to Benin City, were informed that regular passenger vehicles would commence operations the following morning, whereas goods vehicles operate all the time and would be able to accommodate all four of us and get us to Benin before dawn. Mama Benin settled for the goods lorry, and shortly after midnight, one was available loaded with large jute bags containing cocoa beans; Mama Benin sat in front with the driver while Albert, Florence and I sat at the back on top of the bags. Florence and Albert faced the back but were comfortably seated, while I was seated on another bag facing them hemmed in by the tailboard of the lorry. The driver's assistant, usually called 'apprentice' because he was in training learning on the job how to drive as well as motor vehicle maintenance, perched himself somewhere near me, sitting for a few minutes and then standing and holding on to the roof of the lorry for another few minutes. His duty was to be on the alert and be ready to respond to instructions shouted down by the driver. One such common instruction was to jump down holding his big wedge of wood and walking behind the lorry when climbing a steep hill (to prevent the lorry from rolling backwards). Albert Florence and I chatted for a while and then presumably dozed off; this would have been about an hour of our estimated two hours' journey. There was a bang and I did not know what happened until it was later recounted to me in the General Hospital Benin City.

The time would have been around 2 am and the driver had called the apprentice to take over the driving from him so the driver could snooze for a short break. After the apprentice had driven for about ten to fifteen minutes, the vehicle meandered to the right and then to the left before heading into the bush, crashed against a big tree and then bounced into another tree before coming to a stop. I had been thrown out of the vehicle and Albert and Florence shouted and cried until Mama Benin and the driver went to meet them at the back of the wrecked vehicle, Mama Benin also crying and praying aloud to God Almighty for deliverance. Passing by vehicles stopped and their drivers and passengers came out with torch lights to see how they could help. I was found in the bush, and brought out to the roadside in an unconscious state. When a vehicle going to Benin that could hold all four of us became available, we were taken to Benin City directly to the General Hospital where I was immediately admitted for medical attention.

It may have been after about two hours or so that I regained consciousness, opened my eyes and asked Mama Benin why she was crying and where I was. She was overjoyed and then danced and praised God for my coming back to life. My recovery continued steadily and the Doctor reassessed me and told Mama she could take me home; I was discharged. We went home, said prayers and then sent a message to our friend and Pastor Reverend Smith to let him know what had happened. Subsequently, everything went well and a few days later, I proceeded to GCI to resume school. All that is just over half a century ago, and now belongs to history as part of forgotten days!

Classes, Classmates and Staff

The Second World War ended in the middle of 1945 and Government College did not waste any time in arranging to return to its home premises at Apata Ganga, the German interns having been removed even before the war ended. The Germans left a souvenir behind; they had planted a street name sign labelled 'Unter der Linden' at either end of the footpath through the orchard and linking Grier House and Swanston House. I later came to know that Unter der Linden is a well-known motor highway in Germany.[Sketch 6]

We called our time away from Apata Ganga as our period in exile. Woodwork and metalwork os had been sustained while 'in exile' by taking the senior students in weekly rotation and batches in a goods truck without seats, every Wednesday to and from the

Apata Ganga site for one and half hour sessions. Things became much easier for these students after the war.

One aspect of life in the College that was totally suspended during 'exile' was swimming. Our permanent site had a well-constructed swimming pool and as soon as the 'exile' was over, the authorities did not hesitate to rehabilitate it and restore the standing order that every student must learn to swim within their first three months (i.e. the first term, January - March) at college. Every year, there was an Inter House Swimming Competition and the general public was usually invited to the final day programme, when prizes and trophies were awarded. I had the honour of being the Grier House Captain of Swimming and of Cricket in my final year in 1946. I was pretty good at both sports and Grier House won both trophies that year.

The academic programme for GCI students was based on a six-year course leading to the Senior Cambridge Examination of Cambridge University England. A pass, in Grade 1 or Grade 2 but not Grade 3, qualified the student to apply to London University for exemption from London Matriculation Examination. In those days a pass in the University of London Matriculation Examination, or exemption from it, we were informed, qualified a candidate for admission to most universities in the United Kingdom, without further examination. By mid-1945, GCI authorities conceded that students by the end of their 5th year were academically up to the Senior Cambridge Examination standard and thenceforth it became an official policy that all students in Class 5 could register for the examination. Hence in 1945, both Class 5 (my class) and Class 6 students registered for and took the examination. The results were very good as most students obtained Grade 1 and 2. In a way, this new policy created some sort of problems for the College authorities, namely what to do with my class in the following year. The programme organised for us that year included exposure to and training in surveying and we were fascinated to use a theodolite. We used it to level the sports field. We also did book-binding techniques and an introduction to bookkeeping and commerce. The latter was of interest because the Bachelor of Commerce was a popular degree in those days, obtainable from London University by correspondence courses. Some of us including me expressed our desire to write an examination in October 1946 – the entrance examination to the Higher College, Yaba. This College was established by the Nigerian Government about 1934 as a post-secondary "institution" to train students in Education and also ran preparatory programmes for various professions such as Engineering and Medicine. When the results of the Senior Cambridge Examination came out, students who were not interested in going on to Higher College went instead to banks to train as bankers, to the Post and Telegraph Department (P&T) as trainee technicians, or to the School of Pharmacy (where they trained for three years to become Registered Pharmacists). Later on, GCI established a two-year programme for the Higher School Certificate, success in which qualified the students for Direct Entry into Nigerian universities.

In my childhood days, I was always fascinated by gadgets and mechanical contrivances, trying to understand how they functioned. Sometimes I dismantled them just to see if I could reassemble them. Sometimes I succeeded, sometimes I failed. I also was attracted to motorcycles and had a strange notion that only engineers rode motorcycles. Because of that I fancied becoming an engineer later in life. However, my sister Mercy, on leaving primary school went to train as a nurse at Iyi Enu Hospital, Onitsha, and she spoke to me on several occasions about her admiration for the doctors at her hospital, their manners, politeness, neatness and their generally kind approach to patients and people. I liked the sound of this and decided to work hard to enter Higher College and to read medicine. When I subsequently told Baba and Mama about my aspiration, Mama heaved a great sigh but said nothing while Baba calmly said that if it was the will of God for me, God would make it possible. I recognised the basis of Mama's quietness and Baba's cautious rejoinder; simply put, it was **"Can we finance such a training?"**

It is interesting to recall at this stage some of the students at the GCI, who became personal friends and also about some of the staff, during my time there.

In my class, I was friendly with Theophilus Ajakaiye who later changed his surname to Obadan; on leaving the college, he worked with Radio Nigeria (later Nigerian Broadcasting Corporation) in the accounting department and became the Chief Finance Officer. He married my cousin Rosebud Usidame, a fully trained nurse and midwife.

Ademola Aderemi, my classmate, the son of the reigning Ooni of Ile Ife, a very good friend, later studied medicine. Years later, we were together again at the Royal College of Surgeons, Lincoln's Inn Fields, London, in a class for tuition revision for the Primary Fellowship Examination, I for Surgery, and he for Ear Nose & Throat specialties.

Ezekiel Bolarinwa, my classmate and an Ibadan citizen, my very good friend, later changed his surname after a few years in the college, to Omitola. On leaving Government College, he joined the Nigeria Police Force, and rose to the rank of Assistant Inspector General of Police by the time he retired from service.

Christopher S O Akande, my classmate, came from Arigidi in Akoko district of Ondo State. He studied Engineering in London where we met again and interacted often when I went to complete my medical studies in London. On return to Nigeria, he took up an appointment with the Western Nigeria Region as a Civil

Engineer; he later became the Head of Service to the Western Nigeria Government.

D C C Ijomah, a very good friend, on leaving the college, worked with Posts & Telegraph Department in the Nigeria Civil Service.

D W I Aluko from Ilesha was a class 3 student when I entered Government College, and in Grier House; we were good friends and later met again in London where he was a student of Engineering at Queen Mary College, later transformed into a University. We ex-GCI students often called him by his initials 'DWI', his full name being Daniel Washington Ibiyemi. Years later back in Nigeria, he encouraged me and my wife to endeavour as soon as was possible, to build our own home in Lagos, and not to rely on living in Government Quarters; this was very useful, sound and timely advice.

Olufemi Olutoye, the son of a School Headmaster in Benin City, and a good family friend came into GCI two years after me. Later pursuing Education, he went to Cambridge University, England, and on his return to Nigeria, joined the Nigerian Army, rising to the rank of General before he retired. While in the army and as a General, he served in the Military regime as a Minister. He later became a traditional ruler, the Alani of Idoani in Akoko district of Ondo State.

There were some students senior to me who on hearing my name and recognising where I came from, introduced themselves to me. These included E E Eboreime, from Afuze; J W A Ohiwerei, from Ora, both final year students; M O Imana, from Ozalla near Ora, who was in his fourth year. All three of them had attended the same primary school in Sabongida-Ora as my eldest brother Alfred. They made me feel at ease in the College just as Donatus Ijomah had done on my arrival.

Mention must be made of a student from Benin City, one year senior to me, in Grier House, who was in Arubayi dormitory with me. He was quiet and inclined to be friendly with all, and was also an all-round good sportsman. In his final year, he was appointed Prefect and did not hesitate to enforce discipline quietly as and when it became necessary. His name was Solomon I Akenzua, the heir apparent to the Benin throne. After leaving Government College, he took on administrative appointments before going to University of Cambridge, England. He returned to Nigeria after graduating, served as Administrative Officer, (District Officer, and later Resident Officer) and finally rose to the rank of Permanent Secretary in the Nigerian Federal Service. He ascended to the throne of Benin Kingdom in 1979 as Oba Erediauwa I.

Some of the prefects in my first and second years had an unpopular behaviour of 'raiding' students' lockers for biscuits, bread, roast groundnuts, gari, ovaltine, sugar and tinned milk, commandeering them and then 'politely' saying to the student *"I'm sure you don't mind my having a little of this"*. Whenever they failed in their mission to exact refreshments from the "rank and file" students, they would turn to either Akenzua or Aderemi with what appeared to be genuine politeness and say *"Let us see what you have in your locker today that we can share with you"*. That way their mission was accomplished!

The teaching staff were all loved by the students.

Captain H T C Field, an English man, was the Principal of the college in my first year; he taught English, especially to the new students; his ambition was to help us overcome common errors that we made when writing or speaking English. An example of such an error that all GCI students never forgot is: *"Never say 'he made me to do it'*, it should be *'he made me do it'*. He saw active service in the 1914 -1918 World War in the Army and had retired as Captain. All students referred to him fondly as Baba Job, but not to his face. It was rather embarrassing when, on some occasions, visitors to the college while addressing the student body 'committed' one or more of these common errors in English language, and the students reacted with a hissing sound, leaving the guest speaker perplexed.

V B V Powell, also an English man but much younger than the Principal, was a physical education and sports enthusiast; he also taught us English language. He was the House Master for Grier House in my first year at the College. He wedded his fiancée who came from England, at our College Chapel about 1937 (before my time). He was very active in all the sports in the college, teaching us the correct way to do everything so as to improve our performance. It may be intriguing to younger readers to learn that we also improved our technique by poring over some well-illustrated books in the Library which we read at our leisure.

An Irishman called Laidlaw taught mathematics which I enjoyed. He played cricket very well, carefully defending his wicket, but not usually making the runs, a classic opening batsman. He also played the piano very well and he supervised the piano lessons of members of the Musical Society to which I belonged.

A A E Sagay, a Nigerian, taught Biology. I vividly remember him taking us out of the classroom into the fields and the bush, to pick leaves of different classifications, and to catch butterflies which we 'mounted' after preserving them with chloroform, in order to identify them with precision. He was a close relation of Reverend Smith who had taught me at KCSG, and had been Pastor in charge of St James' Church, Benin City in 1941. At the request of my sister Mama Benin, Reverend Smith gave me a letter of introduction to Sagay. On arrival at Government College, I promptly located him and presented him with the letter. He welcomed me cheerfully and became my mentor during my studentship. The first term ended with the Easter vacation popularly called the April holidays, which lasted three weeks. Those students whose homes (parents' or guardians') were not far, like Lagos,

Abeokuta, Ijebu, Ile Ife, Ilesha, went home, but those whose homes were farther away were allowed to remain in the college. They called themselves April Rainers, an expression we borrowed from the English song 'Green grow the rushes oh'. Sagay invited me to spend my first April vacation with him and his family, and I gladly and promptly accepted the invitation. He and his wife were very good to me and I was very happy. They had a baby son, a few months old, whose name was Itse, and when he grew up became a Professor of Law at Ife University (Obafemi Awolowo University). Later still, we met at the University of Benin where he became the first Dean of the Faculty of Law and I was a Professor of Surgery (Orthopaedics) and the Dean of the School of Medicine. He had a successful legal career and became not only a Senior Advocate of Nigeria (SAN), but also a Special Adviser (Legal) to President Muhammadu Buhari of Nigeria. Before I completed my schooling at GCI, A A E Sagay, was transferred to Benin City to become the Principal of Edo College, Benin City.

After my first year in GCI, I was regularly an 'April rainer'. I loved the April holidays. We had no tuition. We were fed at the same times as during the term. We organised ourselves through a rota to keep the premises clean; and arranged different games, like five-aside football, basketball, cricket in practice nets only, table tennis, playing the piano, chess, draughts and monopoly. Ballroom dancing was gaining popularity in Nigeria about that period and I recall us teaching ourselves the steps from a book on ballroom dancing, authored by Alex Moore (if I remember rightly). The April Rainers were very enthusiastic about ballroom dancing.

Ballroom dancing had come to us from England and gained popularity in the early 1930's. Iin Nigerian villages, crowds would gather in the evenings to participate. While one person knocked an empty tin with a nail or a stone at rhythmic intervals, another would sing and you would hear yet a third person calling out in a loud clear voice,, "slow, slow, quick quick slow" or "one two three, one two three" and so on. These events were called "gran bol" derived from the expression 'grand ball dance'. In cities like Lagos, Ibadan, Port Harcourt, Benin City, Warri, and perhaps others that I did not know, ballroom dancing became so popular that there was an annual Nigerian Ballroom Dancing Competition. On at least one occasion I remember that a former student of GCI, V H A Aneke, a Grierson, won the title. GCI pupils and Griersons in particular were elated. Aneke had graduated from Government College in December 1940, the month before I entered.

Nigerian members of the teaching staff, and there were many, included C A Ekere, from Calabar region who taught Geography, G N I Enobakhare from Benin, an ex-student of GCI, who taught Mathematics, and later served as Principal of GCI, S O Bisiriyu from Abeokuta, an ex-student of GCI, who taught English and a student contemporary of Enobakhare. Bisiriyu would be remembered for a long time by students of the 1940's vintage for his lessons on phonetics: e-du-ca-tion, pronounced as "er-doo-kay-shun" and "op-por-tu-ni-ty" with appropriate up and down intonations. He later changed his surname to Biobaku; obtained a doctorate degree from University of London; was for some time the Liaison Officer for Students in the Students Affairs Department of the Colonial Office in London before he returned to Nigeria, finally becoming Secretary to the Western Nigeria Government.

I recall with nostalgia in 1941/1942, during one of our Saturday evening entertainment sessions how some of the students in the class immediately senior mine enacted a short play about going to the moon, wearing strange garments and headgear which they thought suitably depicted astronauts; it all was great fun in those days and most of us thought entirely impossible and mere science fiction. Yet just about three decades later, Neil Armstrong and colleagues landed on the moon.

Chapter 8

CHANGE, CHANGE, CHANGE

Higher College Yaba

I was successful in the 1946 entrance examination to Higher College Yaba, and duly reported for admission in January 1947. It was encouraging that some of the second-year students at Higher College 1947 (admitted January 1946) had passed the Senior Cambridge Examination with me in 1945 and they were known to me; one of them, Edgal, my cousin, trained in Kings College Lagos; his studies were in the discipline of Education. Some other students were ex-GCI.

Students at Higher College Yaba were taught the preliminary subjects leading to specialties in Education & Teaching, Administration, Finance, Engineering and Medicine; this was organised to make the students employable in the Nigerian Government Civil Service primarily, and then the private sector. One of my seniors at Higher College Yaba in 1947, the elected student leader and student in charge of Religious Affairs was Osinulu S.A. Years later, he became the Prelate of the All Nigeria Methodist Church.

The Nigerian Government had considered reorganising the education system in Nigeria for some years and subsequently developed vocational institutions: Trade Centres for post-primary students, and Technical Institutions for post-secondary students. A fall-out of this broad scheme was that in 1946, the Higher College Yaba was officially re-designated as Technical Institute Yaba. Consequently, when I entered Higher College Yaba January 1947, the two bodies of students and their corresponding staff – members of the older Higher College to which I belonged, and those of the newer Institute, existed side by side and in the same premises; there was no interaction academically between them, and the staff were different. The Institute slowly and doggedly established itself and its programmes for the technical students and it was obvious that the original Higher College was being phased out. The concept of the Technical Institute was the forerunner of Polytechnics and Colleges of Technology that developed in later years. The Technical Institute Yaba was later renamed The College of Technology Yaba.

First medical students at University College, Ibadan

Then came December 1947. The Department of Education arranged a special dinner for Higher College students, attended by the Education secretary herself (equivalent to the current grade of Federal Minister of Education). She bid farewell to the 2nd year and other senior students, and then to the 1st year students (my set), said ***"We hope to meet again soon in January 1948 at Ibadan, where you will be foundation students of University College Ibadan, an integral College of University of London"***. What a thrill and delight, as there was at that time no university in Nigeria; in fact, the only degree-awarding institution in the four British-administered territories in West Africa comprising Nigeria, Gold Coast (later Ghana), Sierra Leone and Gambia was Fourah Bay College, in Freetown in Sierra Leone, and most of its degrees were related to Religious Studies.

In January 1948, I went to the University College in Ibadan, accommodated in a collection of wooden buildings previously occupied and used by the military garrison. I soon linked up with fellow students from Yaba. After due registration at the administration office, I was led to my room, with bed and locker. The Head of Administration of University College was the Principal, Dr Kenneth Mellanby, while the other significant administrative officer was the Warden, Mr Lambert. The administrative office building and the buildings for Dining Hall and Common Room looked obviously like recent additions following vacation by the military garrison. The student body was made up of all who transferred from Higher College Yaba as well as students from the Survey School, Oyo, making an overall student population of 103. However, I have seen some publications in the last decade or two, claiming that there were 104 students at the inception of University College Ibadan.[17]

The academic focus of the University College initially was to ensure that all 'Yaba' students could continue their preliminary studies for London University's Intermediate B.A. or B.Sc Examinations. The first examination was held in June 1948, and the successful students proceeded to register for the Bachelor degrees as internal students of University of London in their respective subjects. All the students in my set who had registered for Medicine and had passed the Inter B.Sc. Examination in the requisite four subjects - Physics. Chemistry, Botany and Zoology, transferred to Lagos in September 1948 to the School of Medicine, Yaba, to commence our studies for the University of London 2nd M.B.B.S. Examination of 1950, (after a two-year course). In November 1948, arrangements were made for us to return briefly to Ibadan to attend the Foundation Laying Ceremony of University College of Ibadan on 17th November, 1948, the Guest of honour being Sir Arthur Creech Jones, Secretary of State for the Colonies, from the United Kingdom. Sir Arthur, in his address, spoke for over an hour without any notes in his hand and I was very much impressed. It reminded me of what I had read in my secondary school days, about the history of England and the British Empire, concerning the filibustering orations of members of the British House of Parliament on vital issues about a century or so earlier. [15][16]

The School of Medicine, Yaba

The School of Medicine, Yaba, had been established in the early 1930's by the Nigerian government, to accept from Higher College Yaba, students who had successfully completed preliminary studies in the four basic sciences of Botany, Zoology, Physics and Chemistry; the School offered tuition in Human Anatomy and Physiology, Biochemistry and Pharmacology in a two-year programme after which the successful students proceeded to the General Hospital, Lagos for Clinical Training. This was the standard medical training programme in Pathology, Medicine, Surgery, Paediatrics, Obstetrics & Gynaecology, and Public Health, lasting three years (longer for repeat examination students). The successful students were then registered by the Government as Doctors but with the designation of Assistant Medical Officers. For any doctor in Nigeria in those days to be designated as a Medical Officer on graduation, he had to have a British or American medical qualification. Hence, some of the Yaba trained doctors travelled to Britain, registered for appropriate intensive training lasting only three to six months, and sat for the appropriate Conjoint Board Examinations to acquire the Licentiate of one of the Royal Colleges of London, Edinburgh, Glasgow or Dublin. As a credit to the training scheme in Nigeria, most of the Yaba doctors who went to Britain returned in about three to six months, having successfully acquired the Licentiate to become registrable as Medical Officers on returning to Nigeria. Occasionally, one or two of them remained longer in the United Kingdom to study and obtain locum jobs in hospitals as appropriate to their disciplines; they sat for the relevant postgraduate examinations of the Royal Colleges and passed, and so obtained the Diploma such as FRCS (Fellow of the Royal College of Surgeons), and MRCP (Member of the Royal College of Physicians). This meant that on the return of these brilliant and hard-working Yaba doctors, those in the civil service were upgraded to full Medical Officers, and in addition, those who had acquired additional training and specialist diploma were promoted to the rank of "Specialist" (equivalent to the Consultant in today's terminology).

With the establishment of University College Ibadan, it took over the Yaba School of Medicine, and the admission of students into the School of Medicine then became officially based on the acquisition of the Intermediate B.Sc. pass in Physics, Chemistry, Botany and Zoology of the University of London. This was also considered to be equivalent to the Higher School Certificate examination. On this premise, the first intake of students (my class) to the School of Medicine, Yaba, as part of University College Ibadan, included some students who had been my seniors in GCI and other Colleges. Two had even been teachers of the girls in my class in their secondary school days. Consequently, we always showed these "senior classmates" reasonable respect in and out of the classroom. Some of the Lecturers were new appointees who came from the United Kingdom, Professor Alastair Smith (Anatomy), Professor Parsons (Physiology), Dr Hendry (Biochemistry), Dr Lin (Pharmacology), and F. O. Dosekun, B Sc (Physiology).[18]

The existing technologists in Anatomy and Physiology, both Nigerians, were retained. Oh what a formidable team! And they all taught us 'with a vengeance' so to speak, as the Professors said **"to bring us up to British Universities' 2nd M.B. standard"**, which they did. Additional staff were recruited as time went on. I remember in particular Dr James Waribo Cookey-Gam, a product of Yaba School of Medicine.[14]

Some years earlier, he had won prizes during his training and was appointed as Lecturer in Physiology a few years after he had graduated.[13] They were all dedicated, competent, pleasant and devoted teachers. One British physiology technologist was recruited by Professor Parsons because as the Professor said, *"he can even cannulate the pancreatic duct of a dog almost with his eyes shut"*.

Clinical training In Ibadan

Time moved on and the 1950 2nd M.B. B. S. University of London examination came and went. The results came from London, and 12 out of 18 of us passed in all subjects; some were referred in one subject each, and one or two failed outright. The successful students were informed and requested to report in Ibadan at the end of the vacation of the University College, to commence clinical training. This was to take place in Adeoyo Hospital, the Native Authority Hospital in Ibadan in preference to the anticipated General Hospital (owned and run by the Nigerian Government). Adeoyo Hospital was in a better shape and standard, equipment wise, than the Government General Hospital in Ibadan; a possible alternative was the European Hospital which was better staffed and better equipped than both the General Hospital and the Native Authority Adeoyo Hospital, but it was avoided perhaps due to political sensitivities because its patients were European or senior Nigerian Civil Servants and it may have been considered improper for them to be used in training. A Teaching Hospital for the University was built after I had left. Its name is the University College Hospital Ibadan and it has retained its premier position in educating doctors and nurses in Nigeria and West Africa. It took some years to build, and it incorporated a School of Nursing & Midwifery.

New clinical and academic staff were recruited to join the existing clinical staff of Adeoyo Hospital. One of these was Professor Jolly, Professor of Surgery, a woman and British citizen who was the author of a standard textbook of Surgery for undergraduates, and we all owned a copy. Other new staff included Dr H.O. Thomas, a Lecturer in Surgery and a Nigerian citizen who had spent many years in England and was a Fellow of the Royal College of Surgeons of England; Professor Alexander Brown, Professor of Medicine, a British citizen; and Professor A.O.Ajose, Professor of Public Health, a Nigerian citizen.

While our Year 1 clinical class programme went on steadily, the 'Yaba students' who were in Clinical Year 2 and Year 3 classes were brought from Lagos General Hospital to join us at Ibadan; they resided with us and the other faculty students of the University College in the former military wooden blocks, each student with his own room. There was a block of rooms for female students of different faculties, widely separated from the main blocks which were for male students. The medical students, pre-clinical, and clinical, were in one block, not mixed up with students from other faculties, and Final Year medical students (Yaba trainees) occupied one end of the block for medical students.

I remember one of the Final Year Students, Diete-Spiff (who after graduation changed his name to Diete-Koki) very well. He came from a wealthy background from what is now known as Bayelsa State. He spoke with a calm friendly voice, was almost always unflappable, dressed neatly (for the average Nigerian), and he had a gramophone with a loudspeaker; when he played the records on his gramophone, usually in the evenings after his day's routine at Adeoyo hospital, or as was more often the case, just before dawn when every student was waking up and getting ready for the day's programme the music came loud and clear to every one of us many rooms away from his; no one objected as far as I recollect, as he seemed to have chosen the time of play reasonably well, and the music was generally acceptable to all tastes.

The senior clinical students from Lagos General Hospital completed their training and graduated as Assistant Medical Officers.

Another exciting episode I cannot forget during my First Clinical Year at Adeoyo Hospital Ibadan was when Professor Jolly saw a young female patient with a large deforming swelling of the lower jaw which the Professor told us was a cancer which was susceptible to radiation therapy. We were fascinated, and eagerly listened to her as she said with confidence that she would arrange the radiotherapy "right here in Ibadan" – a concept that was bewildering beyond our imagination. And she did. By careful, well planned and coordinated schedules involving phone calls, and arrangement for ambulance services, radio-active "needles" were ordered from England, brought by air to Lagos Airport in sealed lead containers, and transported by well-briefed staff from Lagos Airport to Adeoyo Hospital Ibadan where the theatre staff, all wearing lead aprons, were waiting to receive the radioactive package. The theatre was ready about an hour before arrival and the operation was carried out immediately, implanting the radioactive needles in the tumour. All the students and the resident doctors, as many as the theatre could accommodate came to watch. We were filled with admiration for the procedures and began the long wait in expectation of the result of this most fascinating operation, an operation that in itself did not take long, perhaps about half an hour, because of having to handle everything with care and caution. After about a week, some reduction of swelling became observable, then as the days went by, there was no doubt about the improvement. The weeks went by, and then the face began to look like a 'normal' face. Yes, the radioactive therapy worked and the patient got better and was discharged from hospital. I cannot now recall for how long the follow-up was, but it was published in a medical journal and can be traced. I was particularly impressed, and as the first patient I clerked in my medical posting was a middle-aged man, diagnosed with primary cancer of the liver, I hoped that he also might be subjected to implantation of radioactive radium needles; unfortunately, my teachers said that the primary cancer of the liver was not sensitive to radiotherapy.

My first year of clinical training was very interesting, as we were introduced to the principles of the practice of clinical medicine coupled with the study of pathology. We were also exposed to post-mortem examinations. Sooner than I expected, as always seems to be the case when a programme is interesting, fascinating and well executed, the first clinical year came to an end and there was a short holiday break of a few weeks, perhaps a month.

Impending radical change

We were aware that a visiting team from University of London had come to see, examine and assess the facilities in Adeoyo Hospital, to enable them to submit a comprehensive report to the Senate of London University. My mind went over previous 'educational assessments' announced by the Nigerian government to decide if, where, and when university level of education should be introduced ; the process leading to a conclusive report and recommendation usually took some years, and the government took perhaps as long to decide what to do. Therefore my fellow students and I were astounded when we received the news within a few weeks that the London University Visitation Report was out. When made public, the report said among other things that the facilities provided at Adeoyo Hospital Ibadan were not acceptable for training students like myself for the M.B.B.S. degrees of London University. More surprising was that the visitors recommended that all students in my class be enabled to go to London to complete our studies. And the greatest surprise of all, was that the Nigerian Government agreed to grant all twelve of us a Nigerian Government scholarship.

Chapter 9

GOING TO ENGLAND

When I went into boarding school at Igarra in 1939 to complete my primary school education, there was time enough for my mother to think it over, sulk for a while and wonder how her little Felix at age 11 years would survive the ordeal of boarding school life, first time away from home. By the time I went to secondary school two years later in Ibadan, located over two hundred miles away by road from where my parents lived, there had not been any significant emotional adjustment. Baba was thrilled and delighted while Mama just accepted everything in good faith, trusting that God was in control of our lives and destiny, especially since Almighty God had seen me happily through six years in GCI and four more years of post-secondary and University education in Lagos and Ibadan. It was bewildering that Felix was now going far, far away to England! Baba was overjoyed, and Mama immediately recalled that Baba was in regular correspondence with Rev. Canon Jebb who had retired from the CMS service in Nigeria and had returned home to England. Perhaps Baba would send a letter to Rev. Canon Jebb requesting him to help keep an eye on Felix. The Rev. Canon Jebb and Baba had worked together for years and a close friendship had developed between them. On his retirement and return home to England, Rev. Canon Jebb sent magazines, journals and bible reading guides to Baba. Looking back now I believe that Rev. Canon Jebb most likely arranged for and paid to have Baba on the mailing list of C.M.S. Headquarters in London. Air mail service in those days was expensive, hence most mails were conveyed by sea and the mail boats took two weeks to travel from Liverpool to Lagos (and vice-versa). Allowing a few days to a week for sorting out mails before despatch within Nigeria, post took about four weeks to reach its destination. Sometimes, movement within Nigeria was hampered by bad roads, or transport problems and the delivery period could be up to about six weeks. This was something I had got used to in the few years of post-secondary education when we students ordered textbooks from Britain.

Things moved rapidly as one event led to the other; letters from University College Ibadan and the Nigerian government informed us, the recipient students of the awards, to be prepared to proceed to Britain; the preliminaries had to be completed quickly, such as going to Lagos to obtain passports, the arrangement for yellow fever vaccination, having medical examination including chest x-rays and obtaining British currency. Our books and any heavy personal effects were to be despatched in trunk boxes by ship as we would be travelling by air so as to meet the deadline for our admission to the University of London's new academic session, beginning in October 1951.

The British Council in Lagos arranged a brief orientation programme for us, the twelve students, a series of talks on the people we were going to live with in Britain, how they behave generally, and any striking differences between living in Britain and living in Nigeria, the foods we would be introduced to, most of which would be different from our common and traditional Nigerian foods; the British Council Officer elaborated on the wearing apparel especially considering that the weather in Britain was significantly much cooler than in Nigeria; we were advised to carry with us very few woollen garments from Nigeria as such garments were generally not the best nor the most appropriate; it was better we should get there and purchase what each one of us individually considered was appropriate. At the time we were going to travel, September ending, the officer said we would not experience any dramatic weather change on arrival in London, being autumn, and there would be time enough to adjust as winter approached. We would all be received by the British Council on arrival in London unless any of us had private arrangements for accommodation.

Within the few weeks of knowing we would go abroad and the travelling date, my eldest sister Mama Benin knitted for me a pair of gloves and a sleeveless pullover. While in Lagos for the travel formalities, I was taken to a tailor who made me a tweed jacket and two pairs of worsted wool trousers, and I was confident I had all that was necessary to cope with the winter that I had heard so much about.

I bought a metal trunk box and packed all my textbooks, a pair of pillow cases, well embroidered by my sister and traditional clothes to wear on occasion to remind me of home. The trunk box was taken to Elder Dempster Shipping Line, to be shipped to England; it would go to Liverpool and then overland by van or by rail to London, all in about three weeks. I therefore packed a small suitcase to hold articles of clothing and a few books to travel with me on the aeroplane. These would suffice in the few weeks before my trunk box arrived.

Welcome to London

Come departure date and my big sister Mama Benin accompanied me to Ikeja Airport, Lagos arriving there about midday. All the other students and their relations were also at the Airport departure lounge where we met, and exchanged pleasantries while some relations shed tears at the impending separation from loved ones. By about 1:00 pm the boarding call sounded and we said our final farewells and boarded the propeller-driven aircraft. About half an hour later, the plane took off. There was a stop-over at Kano airport in the late afternoon, and another stop in North Africa in the middle of the night.

By dawn the pilot announced we were circling over Paris and about 45 minutes later, we circled over London and then came down at about 8:00am at London Airport. Meals had been served during the flight, a snack and drink on take- off from Ikeja airport, a good meal hours later between Kano and the North African stop-over; then a light breakfast was served just before landing at London airport. We were received at the airport by a British Council official who took us to the British Council transit lodge in Notting Hill Gate, travelling on the underground train and when we got there we relaxed for the rest of the day.

The next day, we vacated the transit lodge; the only female student in our group was taken to the London University Hostel for women near Russell Square. Ayodele Onifade was collected by his cousin Akinola Aguda who was a law student in London living in private accommodation, and the remaining ten of us took the underground trains again, this time to Knightsbridge, to the Colonial Students Centre at No. 1 Hans Crescent, Knightsbridge, in Central London. Mr Lambert, warden for students' affairs at University College Ibadan was waiting to receive us and settle us in the hostel after a brief talk introducing us to London and England in general. If I recall rightly, it was about then that we received individual packaged information regarding the details of our respective medical schools, dates of registration, and how to reach our schools by bus or by underground trains; the London Transport maps for visitors to London were also provided.

In the evening of that day if I remember rightly, he came and took us to watch a fantastic sporting event at the White City Stadium, under floodlights.

We were distributed to twelve different medical schools in London, every one of them an integral part of the University of London. I recall the names of the schools (and students) with nostalgia as follows, in alphabetical order: (Fig 24: The twelve of us with Dr Hendry, our biochemistry teacher in Nigeria)

Charing Cross Hospital Medical School   OKUNGBOWA Gabriel (ex- St Gregory's College, Lagos)

Guy's Hospital Medical School   ORHEWERE Felix (ex- Government College Ibadan)

King's College Medical School   AUDU Ishaya

St Bartholomew's Hospital Medical School   AKINLA Oladele (ex- Government College Ibadan)

St George's Hospital Medical School   ONIFADE Ayodele (ex – Government College Ibadan)

St Mary's Hospital Medical School   NGU Victor Anoma (ex – Government College Ibadan)

St Thomas Hospital Medical School   OGBEIDE Michael (ex – Government College Ibadan)

The London Hospital Medical College   GEORGE S. Afolabi (ex – Government College Ibadan)

The Middlesex Hospital Medical School   NWABUOKU Eugene

The Royal Free Hospital Medical School   SODIPE Wuraola, Miss (ex - CMS Girls School, Lagos)

The Westminster Hospital Medical School   UDEOZO I.O. Kanayo

University College Hospital Medical School ERUCHALU Raphael O.C. (ex – Dennis Memorial Grammar

School, Onitsha)

It was quite an experience travelling on the London Underground. I had got used to travelling by train in Nigeria since I entered GCI in 1941, where the "original model steam engines" were required to stop at every station "to drink water" so as to generate the steam to carry the train to the next station. I had seen films of electric powered train engines moving fast and relatively quietly, but above ground. However, the concept of a train carrying hundreds and perhaps even thousands of people while diving into the ground like a rabbit entering its burrow and later resurfacing at a distance far from its entry point, was mind-boggling. How was rain water kept from flooding the network of tunnels of these trains? How was enough fresh air made available for the passengers inside these 'shut-up' trains deep down under the earth's surface? What about the fear of possible electrocution? So many questions came to my mind, but I remained "brave" and did not let anyone know that it took a lot of courage and determination for me to venture into these underground 'journeys'. In barely a week, I had overcome these feelings, and in another week or so I was among those who would run down the stairs, not walk, if my train was thundering into the station, so as not to miss it.

Harrods Ltd & Hans Crescent Students' Centre

Within a few weeks, it dawned on us that Knightsbridge where our hostel was located is one of the most expensive districts in London. The building we stayed in is still there. Just two doors away from our hostel was a massive multi-storey building at the junction of Hans Crescent and Knightsbridge, the world famous department store called Harrods. Within a few days of my arrival I made time to wander around the various departments on the different floors of Harrods; it seemed to me a large shop designed to cater specially for 'royalties, celebrities and the rich', in view of the way its immaculately dressed, polite sales attendants spoke with in alluring low-tones, almost inviting one to part with every penny or rather pound in one's wallet; and then there were the thick pile carpets on the upper floors encouraging customers to relax and experience the joy of spending money. The music department had every conceivable kind of musical instrument, and I was particularly attracted to the special rooms designed for listening to music undisturbed by the noise from the rest of the shop. These soundproofed rooms had well-cushioned seats for customers to sink into while they played a record or two in order to make a choice: to buy or not to buy. Any particular record a customer enquired about that was not available could be ordered from the recording company, to be delivered within a week. After all, the store's telegraphic address was 'EVERYTHING LONDON'. Harrods also prided itself in claiming that whatever a customer required from any part of the world, if not available in the store, could also be ordered and delivered by a specified date, costs and expenses being quietly and calmly referred to only as a matter of polite conversation.

Our Hans Crescent residence, as a former 4 or 5-star hotel before the Second World War, had wonderful facilities to offer entertainment for its residents; a large hall that could accommodate about two hundred or so guests and a stage for acting. Music recitals, lectures, debates and ballroom dances were all held there. The dances, usually held on Saturday nights, were very popular with the students. Ballroom dancing was not strange to me; the colonial administrators had introduced it to Nigeria early in the twentieth century, and by the end of the First World War, it had caught the fancy of many Nigerians, spreading from towns like Lagos, Port Harcourt, Calabar, Warri on the coast inland. Rhythm is innate in most Africans and their music, and with Africans forming the majority of residents in Hans Crescent the organisers often invited orchestral bands that could play rhythmic music in addition to the conventional tunes of the waltz, foxtrot, quickstep; the students favoured the Tango, Samba, Conga, West African highlife, and the ever-popular Caribbean Calypso. In Britain, and especially in London in the early years after World War II, centres flourished for ballroom dancing in the afternoons, about 3pm to 6pm, most often patronised by young men and women, typically students aged 20 to 35 years. To complement the available opportunities and venues for social relaxation and entertainment, the British Council was not left out. It had a centre that provided organised activities especially for overseas students in Britain, in their leisure hours or days. One of the activities that I liked and registered for was Scottish traditional dancing, and I believe I did very well at it. I attended music recitals of the works of the classical composers such as Mozart, Beethoven and others to which I had been introduced in GCI, from time to time at the British Council Centre. The Council also arranged affordable holiday tours especially packaged for overseas students to different parts of the United Kingdom of Great Britain and Northern Ireland, to enable us to learn about the people, their customs, lifestyles and even their history and so enjoy our stay.

The main goal

Following our arrival in London, we duly registered in our respective medical schools, and commenced our clinical training. The routine was comparable in all the medical schools, as we found out when we exchanged views in the evenings. We had the usual lectures and demonstrations, attended outpatient clinics to learn from the consultants and senior registrars, attended ward rounds; and clerked patients in the wards assigned to us, just as we had been trained to do at Adeoyo Hospital. Each of the medical schools also encouraged students to find time for sports like football, cricket, rugby, swimming, tennis, hockey and any others as fancied; these were organised by students themselves. There were also facilities for theatrically talented students. At Guys, academic programmes on Wednesdays ended by 1.00 pm, to enable students to pursue the sport they were interested in. There was a swimming pool in the basement of the lecture-block annexe, open every day from 9 am to about 8 pm, and a squash court. I liked swimming and I went swimming from time to time, either in the mornings on those days when lectures commenced at or after 10 am, or at the end of the day after 6pm before returning to my hostel.

David Ofomata, a Nigerian, was a medical student at Guys (this was the appellation used instead of the full title, Guy's Hospital Medical School) senior to me, and he loved playing squash and tried to interest me in the game; I found it rather too fast and vigorous and so did not follow it up. He had a cheerful disposition, we became good friends, and he was loved by many students. David graduated in 1954 and returned to Nigeria, setting up what later became a very successful medical practice in his home town Nnewi in what is today Anambra State.

G L Monekosso, a Cameroonian, was a clinical student senior to me; he had been my senior at Higher College Yaba in 1947. On graduating in 1953, he gave me some of his textbooks and returned home.

Ola Fajemisin, who had been two years senior to me at Government College Ibadan had worked in Nigeria for a few years before deciding to study medicine abroad; he too was at Guys in his pre-clinical studies when I entered Guys. While In GCI, his classmates usually addressed him as "Ola-Faj". After graduating, he specialised in Obstetrics & Gynaecology, and set up a well known Nursing Home in Yaba, where about a decade later, my youngest child was born. An older member of the Fajemisin family, a medical doctor, married my cousin Julie Imoukhuede. Before her marriage she was one of some teachers in training who were posted to GCI for a few weeks for practicals, teaching classes 2B, 2A and class 3 (my class). Students in class 3 resented being taught by female teachers, as it had never happened in our school since its foundation and so they staged a demonstration. This was promptly and firmly quelled and we returned to our lessons. A few months later while the College was still in "exile" along Ijebu Bye Pass, two British female teachers joined the staff as full-time teachers and no demonstration took place.

Frederick Negbenebor was at Guys too, but junior to me. He had been my junior at Government College and was in Grier House. He made history at Guys when the Guys Magazine was published with an editorial titled "CALL ME FRED", based on him being friendly and his willingness to be called Fred rather than his long surname. He later trained as an Obstetrician & Gynaecologist, and went on to set up a successful practice in Benin City, Nigeria. He remained a good friend to me and my family.

Henry Innis-Palmer was another Nigerian student I met at Guys in a pre-clinical class in 1951. After graduating, and on return to Nigeria, he was, at one time, a Medical Officer at the Royal Orthopaedic Hospital Igbobi, joining me and other medical officers already there. He later specialised in Radiology and was appointed Consultant Radiologist based at General Hospital, Lagos. He and his wife of Jamaican parentage became good family friends to me and my wife. Her maiden name was Petgrave.

At Guys, I met another Nigerian student Ogunbiyi, who had gone to Britain to study Medicine as a mature student, having retired from the Nigerian Government Service as Chief Pharmacist (one of his children was a medical student in Cambridge University). We became friends and when I returned from Nigeria to Guys for a course in preparation for the second and final part of the Fellowship Examination in Surgery in 1961, we met again at the Guys cafeteria and he had graduated and had set up himself in General Practice in London; his son had graduated much earlier and was well on his way to becoming a Surgeon with the FRCS diploma, later becoming a Neurosurgeon.

K G Korsah, a Ghanaian, was a pre-clinical student when I entered Guys. After graduation, he trained to become an Orthopaedic Surgeon, returned home and was based in Accra, Ghana. We met again over two decades later in Paris, France, when we were both attending a conference on Rheumatology.

When I was a clinical medical student at Adeoyo Hospital Ibadan, 1950/51 session, I went to stay with my sister, Mama Benin during the vacation. I went to the General Hospital, Benin City and introduced myself to the Doctor in charge requesting his permission to attend his ward rounds, clinics and operation sessions, to learn whatever I could learn; he approved, and I gained very useful knowledge that helped me years later. He married a daughter of Reverend Smith who had been my teacher at Igarra. His name was Dr O B Alakija. A decade later in 1960 when I was a medical officer at Igbobi Hospital, I met him again at Medical Headquarters, Lagos, in the course of making arrangements to return to the United Kingdom for postgraduate studies. He was the Senior Medical Officer (Administrative), and was high up in the hierarchy close to the Chief Medical Adviser to the Federal Government of Nigeria. It was then that he let me know that he trained at Guys and had graduated in the mid-1930's. It's a small world!!

Interestingly, at Guys, there were from time to time, free complimentary tickets from entertainment theatres in the West End of London, posted on the notice board available to those interested; I was very much interested and made good use of these offers to attend matinee performances at 2.00 pm on Wednesdays & Saturdays, or 7.30 pm on other days of the week according to the day on the ticket. In those days there were no performances on Sundays in the West End.

I recall that about January/February 1952, there were posters, billboards on buses, underground trains and open advertisements on radio and television advertising the forthcoming performance of Handel's Messiah at The Albert Hall, London. I booked a seat early in March for the performance due in April at Easter weekend. I had longed for years to have the opportunity some day, to listen and watch a live performance of the complete Handel's Messiah oratorio and I was taking no chances of missing this. Years back when I was at The Higher College, Yaba, in 1947, our Botany Lecturer Dr H J Savory an Englishman often invited us the students who were interested in music, to his residence on Saturday evenings to listen to gramophone records of classical music and grand operas. We went in small numbers, like first eight to ten to arrive, and he usually served us biscuits and orange squash during the social evening. We loved the music and because some of us including me did not always follow the trend of events in the operas, Dr Savory would fill us in with the background story before playing the record. When the University College of Ibadan took over the students of the Higher College, Yaba, Dr Savory went with us to Ibadan for an academic session and then left and took up an appointment at University of The West Indies in Kingston, Jamaica. We missed him very much, not only for these social evenings, and his lectures in botany, but also because he was a good all-round cricketer, batting and bowling (and I love cricket).

My eagerness and enthusiasm to participate in as many of these activities as possible was so strong that it took me the greater part of my first year in London to learn to discipline myself and remember my primary objective for going to London.

Within the same premises as the Medical School was the Guy's Hospital Dental School, and there was a high level of social interaction between their students, medical students, and the students of the School of Nursing & Midwifery. Plays were organised between them, music recitals and performances were held, and weekend parties including dancing took place. The climax of this socialising was at Christmas when the student groups arranged a combined fiesta of eating, drinking, and dancing.

I recall some of the academic staff readily, as they made a significant impact on me and I would like to take a moment to remember them.

Sir Russell Brock, a cardio-thoracic surgeon, had at that time made dramatic surgical advances by his operations on the chest, which earned him world acclaim as well as a Knighthood from His Majesty King George VI of England.

Mr Hedley Atkins was a general surgeon with focus and expertise on disorders of the breast and their surgical management. He was appointed a Professor by University of London, during my studentship, the first Clinical Professor at Guys to be so recognised; until that time, medical Professors at Guys were in non-clinical disciplines such as Anatomy, Biochemistry and Pathology.

Sir John Conybeare, author of a textbook of medicine which practically every student owned a copy, was a very popular teacher. Because he had suffered and survived one or two heart attacks, he usually sat down at the patients' bedside during his weekly grand teaching ward rounds, and every student was allowed to take a chair (folding or any other pattern) to use during his ward rounds.

Dr A H Douthwaite, was the Senior Physician in the 'firm' in which I served my first medical clerkship. I admired him as he was tall, elegant, and always immaculately well dressed.

Mr Sam H Wass was the Senior Consultant Surgeon in the 'firm' in which I served my second surgical clerkship, pleasant, friendly, and a competent surgeon, loved by all his students, and regarded as a wonderful teacher. He was fondly called 'Sammie Wass' by all students who had done surgical clerkship with him, and we loved to join his teaching weekly ward rounds, whether first, second, or third year clinical students.

Dr McArdle was a Senior Consultant Neuro-Physician with whom I served my last medical clerkship before graduating. I was the only student in the 'firm' and I learnt a lot of clinical neurology which has served me very well in my medical career, especially as I became an Orthopaedic Surgeon.

I recall with nostalgia what I regarded as the most fascinating Department at Guys, from an academic point of view. The Gordon Museum was based in a multi-storey building that housed pathology specimens from real patients. Each specimen was clearly mounted in preserving fluid such as formalin, in a glass or plastic container, and there was a detailed write-up of medico-pathological information beside every specimen. Such information indicated whether it was a biopsy, operative, or post-mortem specimen, with the appropriate addition where applicable of symptoms and physical signs on clinical examination, and investigation results. Students invariably made time to spend hours in The Gordon Museum to augment their formal teaching in classrooms, wards, outpatient clinics, operating theatres, post-mortem examinations, departmental meetings and conferences. Some of these specimens were well over a hundred years old and were in a perfect condition of preservation.

After settling into my programme of studies at Guys, I located the Headquarters of the C.M.S. at 6 Salisbury Square, EC2, off Fleet Street, and introduced myself. I was warmly received and given letters of introduction to some members; I was also given a leather-bound copy of the New Testament which I treasure till this day, over seventy years later.

I made contact with my father's friend Rev Canon Jebb and his wife who, some months later, invited me to spend a weekend with them at their home near Hastings, on the south coast. It took me some months to choose a church at which to worship regularly. First, I went to Holy Trinity Church, Brompton, a relatively short walking distance from Hans Crescent Hostel. Then I moved to Southwark Cathedral, which is walking distance from Guy's Hospital, but was a good half hour by underground train from Hans Crescent, with two changes to get to London Bridge Station; This was very 'high church' and seemed to me more like a Roman Catholic service; then I was introduced to St Martin-in-the-Fields Church at Trafalgar Square, very welcoming to students, especially students and visitors from oversea countries; and lastly, I found All Souls Church, Langham Place, about five minutes' walk from Oxford Circus, where I settled. Rev Stott was the priest in charge when I started worshipping there.

As time went on, my close friends from Nigeria, Raphael Eruchalu and Ayodele Onifade got married. Raphael married Caroline who had come from Nigeria a few months before the wedding; they had been friends before we left Nigeria, and Ayodele married Christie, also a Nigerian, who was training as a nurse at the Royal Free Hospital, London. I was Best Man at each wedding. I had met a friend of Christie's and her classmate too at the School of Nursing of The Royal Free Hospital late 1952, but it was about a year later when some attraction developed between us; the attraction grew into a friendship, and we began to desire to see each other more frequently and to know each other better. As time passed by, there was no doubt we were in love. Her name was Claris Ermine Fenton, a Jamaican national, who had come to Britain to study nursing on a Jamaican Government sponsorship. She was based at the Royal Free Hospital, London. She completed her nursing training shortly before I graduated and with the consent of both families, hers being in Jamaica and mine in Nigeria, we got married on 28th May, 1955, at All Souls Church, Langham Place, London; my Best Man was Raphael Eruchalu who having already graduated with distinction in 1954, was offered and had accepted a job as a House Physician at University College Hospital, Gower Street, London where he had trained.[Fig 25]

Chapter 10

LIFE AS A NEWLY QUALIFIED DOCTOR

Housemanship Training

I graduated at the beginning of May 1955 and almost immediately commenced a locum appointment as a House Physician at Lewisham General Hospital, South East London.

I was thrilled and delighted to be addressed as 'Doctor' by patients in the wards as well as in out-patient clinics; Staff Nurses; Nursing Sisters and Matron; other doctors (House officers like me, Senior House Officers, Registrars, Senior Registrars) and also Consultants - Junior as well as Senior. I had truly acquired a name and title that was prestigious and well respected world-wide. I gained a lot of practical experience and confidence in the care of patients, and I am and will forever be particularly grateful to all the Nursing Staff who assisted me by their guidance, reminding me kindly and reassuringly in a friendly manner, that they were aware that I had only just graduated. That was wonderful! The senior and more experienced doctors I worked with also helped me gain experience and confidence, but while they didn't express it, the attitude they displayed left me in no doubt that they were thinking ***"Boy, you've got a long way to go"***. Toward the end of my locum appointment, I applied to various hospitals and without much delay, and after interview, I secured a House Surgeon appointment at St Nicholas' Hospital, Woolwich, South East London; this was a six months appointment in which I served three Consultants: Van Essen in General Surgery, Gabe in Urology, and Lurie in Ophthalmology. On alternate weekends, and alternate Wednesday evenings, I covered for my colleague in the Ear, Nose and Throat Department so she could be off duty, just as she also covered for me on alternate weekends and alternate Wednesday evenings. It was a very pleasant appointment. Van Essen, a white South African national was the friendliest to me of the three consultants; altogether, I enjoyed the six months, seeing my wife in Central London, alternate weekends and half days on alternate Wednesdays.

Towards the end of the appointment in December 1955, I set about securing a new six months appointment as House Physician. I travelled to many hospitals, literally almost all over England in cold, cold winter, for interviews, sometimes travelling by late night trains to arrive at my destination by dawn for a 9am interview appointment. Eventually, I secured a job in the old city of Bath in Somerset, a beautiful quiet city without the noise of traffic that I had become accustomed to in London. My new job was a combined post of three months as House Physician in General Medicine at St Martins' Hospital, Bath, followed by three months as House Physician at the Royal Mineral Water Hospital, Bath, later renamed The Royal National Hospital for Rheumatic Diseases, Bath. I liked my housemanship at St Martins Hospital as I was exposed to a wide variety of clinical problems in medicine and their management. I also recall with pleasant memories that one of the resident doctors, a senior house physician, often entertained us in the residents' sitting room with his set of records of music of Gilbert & Sullivan operettas, usually on Sunday afternoons until dinner was served. The appointment at The Royal Mineral Water Hospital was professionally speaking, more stimulating and challenging. Rheumatology covers a very wide range of disorders capable of disabling the sufferers to varying extents. The hospital was built over ancient Roman baths utilising the natural hot springs for healing, and a Spa had been in the site for many centuries. I was the truly **resident** doctor, residing in a one room flat in the same building as the hospital. The Consultant Physician in charge was Dr John Kersley and we got on very well; he sometimes came to the hospital on ward round days accompanied by his large Alsatian dog. John Bastow, an orthopaedic surgeon and an Australian, came from the Bath & Wessex Orthopaedic Hospital, once a week to review our rheumatic patients to assess if any of them required surgery to improve their health and recovery. Such a patient would be duly prepared and on the agreed date, would be transferred by ambulance to the orthopaedic hospital for surgery and then returned to us at the Mineral Water Hospital. Any patient considered to be seriously in need of special or intensive post-operative care was admitted to the orthopaedic hospital, until he or she was well enough to be brought back. After working for about six weeks at the Mineral Water Hospital, Bastow asked me if I would like to observe my patients being operated on at the orthopaedic hospital. I sought Dr Kersley's permission and he approved. After a few such visits to the orthopaedic hospital, Bastow asked me if at the end of my appointment at the Mineral Water Hospital, I would be interested in an appointment to the Bath & Wessex Orthopaedic Hospital. My face lit up with joy and I said I would. I then put in a formal application for the job, was invited for an interview and I was offered the job. This time there would be no long break looking for another job, writing applications and hoping to be called for an interview. I took up my appointment as Senior House Officer (SHO Orthopaedic) at Bath & Wessex Orthopaedic Hospital for six months, and my wife and I were very happy because we were thereby saved from seeking new accommodation as she and our baby would remain at our rented flat in Bath.

My new outlook

That was how I ventured into the discipline of orthopaedic surgery and practice. There were four Consultant Orthopaedic Surgeons at that hospital. They were Bastow, the administrative head and senior, A E Burton, Tom Price, a Welshman, well-liked by many of us, and Hall, the youngest. Tom Price encouraged me to develop more than a casual interest in orthopaedics and go to University of Liverpool for the degree of M Ch Orth (a Master's degree in Orthopaedics). The other three surgeons had the F R C S Diploma (as for General Surgeons) and then had trained in orthopaedics, training by apprenticeship for several years. While Price was more interested in managing orthopaedic cases, Burton and Hall were more at ease managing only trauma cases, but they did accept and manage any orthopaedic patients that were admitted in emergency under their care. Bastow was at home managing both orthopaedic and trauma cases. Tom Price was very friendly to me and invited my wife and me to his home. At the end of my six months appointment, I did not have difficulty securing another orthopaedic appointment, this time in Southend-on-sea as Senior House Officer (SHO orthopaedic) for a year. Southend being a popular seaside holiday town, most of the patients at Southend General Hospital had trauma (injury) related problems and not primary orthopaedic disorders. To enable me to reside off the hospital premises with my wife and baby, I had to have a means of transport to use when responding to emergency calls. I bought an old bicycle from the second-hand dealer's shop; I used it for a year by which time I decided to return to Nigeria. When I returned it to the dealer's shop with the receipt of purchase I got back the full amount I had paid for it.

Chapter 11

RETURN TO NIGERIA

Arrangements for my return journey to Nigeria went into full swing from September/October 1957. We would travel by ship and not by air. I had requested my cousin in Lagos to ensure a good hotel reservation for us, my wife, myself and our daughter Francine. We embarked on a fourteen days' voyage on the boat "***mv Accra***" of Elder Dempster Shipping Line, from Liverpool and arrived Lagos on the morning of Christmas Eve, December 24, 1957, to be met by our cousin who had visited us in Southend, and who had made the preparations for our accommodation; he was accompanied by my sister Mama Benin and many other family members. It was the tradition in those days, for family and friends to go to Lagos Port to welcome any relation or friend, who had in popular parlance **"gone overseas and returned with the GOLDEN FLEECE"**. What a spectacle! Over twenty people were on the quay to welcome the young student who left in 1951 and was now back home - a qualified Doctor with a wife and child! Furthermore, being the first medical doctor from Ora, the entire Eme and Ora indigenes resident in Lagos, both male and female, wasted no time in organising a grand reception for us, which took place about a fortnight later. (Fig 26: Ora indigenes in Lagos at a reception for me, Jan. 1958) Immediately after the Christmas holidays, I proceeded to Medical Headquarters, Lagos 'to report for duty' The Senior Medical Officer (S M O) who attended to me was flabbergasted when I indicated that I was interested in Orthopaedics, and he promptly phoned the Specialist in charge of Royal Orthopaedic Hospital Igbobi to say *'**there is a crazy young doctor in my office now, who is interested in***

orthopaedics, should I send him to you?' and the Specialist responded by saying ***'right away'***. The SMO then told me ***'you can start tomorrow'*** to which I said that, having been away for some years, I would like to see my parents first. He conceded that I should therefore assume work on 2nd January 1958, barely one week later. I accepted the posting. Accommodation was the next issue to be tackled. I, my wife and our child went to Ora to be reunited with my parents. It was a very short visit and I returned to Lagos, leaving my wife and daughter with my brother Edward and his family at Owo until I had sorted out accommodation in Lagos.[8]

On the boat from Liverpool, we made friends with a young Nigerian couple called Sam and Bessie Ofili, and they came to my rescue regarding accommodation by offering us a bedroom in their Idi-Oro residence. They had a son Ngozi about the same age as our daughter Francine. With accommodation arranged, my wife and Francine returned to Lagos by Armel's Transport, having spent a few weeks in Owo. What a harrowing journey during the harmattan season for my wife and daughter. Coming from England, they found it hot and almost suffocating, but for all the other passengers it was the cold, cold, cold harmattan season and the tarpaulin blinds had to be kept closed to keep off the 'cold' winds or draughts and the red dust!! They arrived in Lagos about 2am, and as the telephone service was limited in those days, they remained at the Armel's terminal in Lagos Island until about 5 am when it was possible to arrange a taxi and we were reunited. We lived with the Ofilis for about six to eight weeks until the Medical Headquarters provided me with a ground floor flat in Igbobi Hospital compound. The Ofilis remained our good family friends.

Igbobi Hospital in the Fifties

The ROYAL ORTHOPAEDIC HOSPITAL, IGBOBI, or as it was popularly called, Igbobi Hospital was a beautifully well laid out hospital in a large expanse of land. It was laid out on the old fashioned principle of large bungalow wards, I remember there were five initially, with wide verandahs to which patients on their beds could be pushed out for sunshine and fresh air as considered necessary. The majority of the orthopaedic patients in the early years were sufferers from tuberculosis of bones and joints. Although it was recognised that their illnesses were not contagious (as compared with pulmonary tuberculosis), the usefulness of ultra-violet rays of the sun was thought to be a high premium. Well to the rear of these bungalow wards was a purpose-built physiotherapy department with the usual facilities to aid patient recovery, and adjoining it was a swimming pool for hydrotherapy, built with donation of funds from the Canadian Government, and officially commissioned by a visiting Royal Personage from the United Kingdom in 1956; thereafter, the hospital was renamed ROYAL ORTHOPAEDIC HOSPITAL; it had previously been known just as 'The Orthopaedic Hospital Igbobi'. At the far back of the hospital was a Workshop for fabricating splints, appliances, some surgical theatre aids, as well as lower limb prostheses, and crutches.

As at January 1958, when I arrived, there were residential quarters for doctors well away from the main hospital complex: a two-storey house for the Specialist-in-Charge; next to that was the bungalow for the Matron-in-Charge Nursing Services; then next was a two-storey block of four flats of which I had been allocated one of the two ground floor flats; and then three two-storey houses that were for other medical officers. These were all linked by a network of macadamised roads along which were Flamboyant Trees, and when they flowered bright reddish-orange, the entire hospital compound was a beauty to behold especially with the 'flame of the forest' look. Many visitors to Lagos often went to see 'Igbobi Hospital' in those days because of its neatness, and beautiful landscape with blooming flowers all the year round. Comparing favourably with the old colonial Ikoyi Park and residences, Igbobi

Hospital was a real tourist attraction for a number of years.

The Royal Orthopaedic Hospital Igbobi as at 1958 was the only orthopaedic hospital in the entire British West Africa, that is Nigeria, Gold Coast (later Ghana), Sierra Leone, Gambia, and the British Cameroons. Kuti, the Officer in charge of the Limb Making & Fitting department in those days, often travelled round these territories to measure and obtain data of patients requiring lower limb prostheses, came back to Igbobi, saw to the fabrications, and then had them fitted under his direct supervision. It seems such a long, long time ago now! Within a few decades, many other orthopaedic hospitals or departments had developed all over Nigeria, government owned as well as private.

Life at Igbobi

The pattern of life in those days was a simple reflection of "Lagos Life", hard work from Monday to Friday, and the weekend for relaxation according to the duty roster for the doctors. Those were the days when as senior civil servants, it was expected that a doctor would engage the services of the following cadres of domestic staff – a house boy or steward, maid, a cook, a driver, a gardener and a nanny if the doctor had a very young child or children; that was the typical profile of a Senior Civil Service Officer as inherited from our colonial masters, except that the "inheritance" was the taste of the individual officer, and not compulsory. My wife and I settled for a house boy only. These domestic staff could be employed directly from the 'Labour Exchange', a government department that often advertised in the local newspapers. I remember an occasion when we engaged a house boy in such circumstances, an indigene from the south-eastern part of the country, and after a month, he said his father was seriously ill and he needed to travel immediately; we allowed him time off and he left. At the weekend, we visited an expatriate friend of ours in Ikoyi, Lagos, who when he wanted to offer us a cold drink called his steward to serve us; to our surprise, it was our houseboy whose father was "**ill**"; he had used the experience gained working with us to apply for a post as steward at a higher wage. That was not an uncommon experience in those days.

Another experience I recollect is when my wife phoned me at work shortly before midday and asked me to come home urgently; fortunately, I was able to go home within half an hour, and my wife said she could not retain the services of the houseboy we had engaged because of his rudeness. She had given clear instructions about some procedure but he preferred to do the job in his own way, and when corrected by my wife, turned round to tell her that he could not tolerate a woman giving him instructions, especially considering that he had two wives at home and neither of them dared to speak to him that way. Needless to say, I paid him off immediately, with additional one month's pay 'in lieu of notice', similar to and in conformity with civil service practice.

The Specialist in charge at Igbobi in January 1958 was Dr. Adewole, an orthopaedic surgeon who had previously practised many years of general surgery in different parts of Nigeria. He was a Fellow of the Royal College of Surgeons of Edinburgh, and had also gone through the University of Liverpool's Orthopaedic Master's degree programme, which Dr Tom Price had spoken to me about in Bath, England when I commenced my orthopaedic career. All other doctors were Medical Officers and we shared the care of patients in rotation through the wards, outpatient clinics, operating theatres and emergency calls. In the operating theatre, we took it in weekly rotation to act as the Anaesthetist, under the watchful eyes of Dr Adewole. In the following two to three years, one by one, most moved away from Igbobi to train as specialists in various medical fields, while other new medical officers were engaged to keep services going. I continued in orthopaedics,

Asekun went into Obstetrics & Gynaecology, Adebonojo into Physical Medicine, Odulate into Ophthalmology, and Innis-Palmer into Radiology. Dr J Waribo Cookey-Gam who had taught me in Yaba School of Medicine was appointed to Igbobi Hospital to take charge of the Physiotherapy Department, and he lived in the second ground floor flat adjacent to me. In the flat directly above me lived Adegunwa, Nursing Superintendent in charge of Operating Theatre, a very pleasant man, who had two wives and a few children; they became very good friends to me and my wife, and they were truly a very happy polygamous family.

Lagos Shopping in the fifties

Life went on smoothly and happily in those days. After the hectic routine from Monday to Friday every week, we often spent Saturday nights visiting the "social night spots" on Lagos Island, dancing from about 9pm till around 1am, and then retiring to our homes. Those night spots usually were known as "TDB, Till Day Break", because the patrons continued merriment, drinking and dancing till about 5am when these venues closed.

Saturday mornings had a special attraction in those days. The Elder Dempster Shipping Line operated ocean liners that plied between the United Kingdom and West Africa on a regular basis. Some ships, like the *mv Aureol, mv Apapa, and mv Accra* were designated as "Mail Boats" because they carried mail in addition to passengers between these countries, and their journeys took fourteen days in either direction, Lagos to Liverpool and vice versa. Other Elder Dempster ships plied the route Lagos to Tilbury, one of the ports on the River Thames, not far from London. The journey lasted three weeks. These were cargo boats, taking on barely about twenty or so passengers, and stopping at every port in West Africa like Lagos, Takoradi, Freetown, Bathurst, to pick up cargo, or to discharge cargo, en route to Tilbury. Passengers on the mail boats travelled either as Cabin Class (standard) or as First Class (which included free alcoholic drinks at all times). Passengers on the cargo boats travelled in the equivalent of First Class, and in those days, they got a real "holiday cruise" and a treat for twenty-one days! My family and I travelled on one of them, the **ss Winneba** from Lagos to Tilbury, when I returned to the United Kingdom for postgraduate studies.

Upper class citizens in Lagos usually expatriate civil servants, but including senior Nigerian civil servants like doctors, engineers, architects, and administrative officers, as well as business tycoons, were familiar with the schedules of the shipping lines so as to keep abreast with when goods and mail would arrive in Lagos. Hence the Saturday after the arrival of a mail boat saw the "celebrities" in Lagos converging on Kingsway Stores; they went there to meet friends for a chat and at the same time to buy many items such as British newspapers and magazines, British assorted vegetables like spinach, cauliflower, cabbage, Irish potatoes, beetroot, poultry and eggs, (there were no poultries developed in Nigeria in those days), beef, chicken, fish, pork, cooked ham, sausages, bacon, clothing, garments, toys, shoes, electrical goods and appliances, cooking oils, teas of different brands, coffee also of different brands, sugar white and brown, cube and granular, and of course alcoholic drinks, beers, cider, gin, whisky, brandy, and tobacco, cigars and cigarettes; in fact, anything and everything exportable from England was made available at Kingsway Stores, an ultra-modern multi-storey Department Store by any standard, with escalators and lifts; it was a branch of the well known United Africa Company, better known as UAC, part of the renowned international conglomerate firm of Unilever. The Cafeteria was the final meeting point where these upper class citizens, while drinking tea or coffee or spirits, reviewed their latest acquisitions and gadgets from overseas. They made sure to let it be known that their purchases came from overseas and were not local, before they gradually dispersed. They would generally only return to Kingsway upon the arrival of the next mail boat. Within a few years, other trading companies like Leventis, UTC and Chellarams, to mention just a few, began to develop comparable department stores, in the hope of attracting similar clientele.

Family Sadness

Early in 1959, my wife and I had a baby boy but he lived only a few months and died. A few months later, my eldest sister Mama Benin came to spend her holidays with us in Lagos, at our Igbobi residence within the hospital premises. She came to commiserate with us over the death of our baby Christopher. Later, she sought medical advice concerning an ailment she had had for some years. After consulting an O & G Specialist, she was admitted to General Hospital Lagos for an operation. Most unfortunately, she died from post-operative complications just a few days after surgery. Her death caused our entire family great distress, especially for me and my wife who had looked forward to her visit to us in Lagos for many months. Worse still, her son Albert, her only child, was at that time a student in Cornell University in New York, U. S. A.; he was alerted as soon as his mother's post-operative condition began to deteriorate, and rushed home. Before he could arrive she had passed away. We travelled together from Lagos to Eme, Ora where her burial took place. Her death was a great tragedy to the entire Orhewere family. The effect on Baba and Mama was profound as Comfort was their eldest child, who had been a confidante to them all her life, and was very much loved by all her siblings. The immediate, urgent and Herculean task that then faced the family was how to console Albert and encourage him to accept that it was absolutely necessary for him to return to his studies in America; to do otherwise would be a great disservice to the honour and memory of his mother. He was emotionally shattered, but by the grace of God, he saw and accepted the wisdom of going back to complete his studies in Cornell University. I am forever grateful to God that Albert not only completed his Master's degree but went on to do doctorate studies. (Photo 9: My nephew Albert, Comfort's son)

In great distress and almost in a confused state of mind, my family and I moved out of our Igbobi hospital residence to seek accommodation away from the hospital environment. That is how we came to dwell in a part of Yaba called Abule Ijesha, somewhere beyond the College of Technology (the old site of Higher College Yaba), in a two-storey building with mathematically designed rows of rooms, upstairs and downstairs, facing one another, with communal kitchen and bathroom and toilet at the rear of each floor, upstairs and downstairs. This style of building was very popular with landlords as it allowed them to maximise the profit from their developments and were called "face me I face you" accommodation. We endured it for only as long as it took us to find something better, about two months, and moved again, to a 4-bedroom bungalow at Moleye Street, Yaba, a self-contained residence with boys' quarters. This was accommodation far in excess of our requirements, and so we were able to offer free accommodation to some of my cousins. Fig 27

It was about this time that my wife took up an appointment as a Nursing Sister with the Military Hospital Yaba, becoming the first non-European and a civilian Nursing Sister to be engaged by the hospital. It was in this capacity that my wife officially represented the nursing services (military) at the celebration for Nigeria's independence at the Lagos Racecourse on the night of September 30, 1960. She was later joined by Mrs Williams as a Nursing Officer at the Military Hospital, Yaba. Late in December 1960, my wife resigned from her job at the Military Hospital to travel with me to the United Kingdom where I went for post-graduate studies and more training in orthopaedics. Mrs Williams went on to do full military training and rose to the rank of Brigadier General (Nursing).

Career Upgrade

The terminology Assistant Medical Officer was gradually withdrawn over a period of years following the establishment of University College, Ibadan, with its Medical School. The vast majority of doctors in the service of the Nigerian Government became Medical Officers by virtue of being University graduates, and progressed with experience over the years to Senior Medical Officer. If and when any of the latter obtained a recognised specialist postgraduate training qualification e.g. the Diploma of the Fellowship of the Royal College of Surgeons, he or she would be upgraded to Senior Hospital Medical Officer, observed for two years and in the absence of any adverse report, would be promoted to Specialist Grade, later renamed Consultant. A doctor who acquired a relevant medical postgraduate degree like a Doctorate or Masters in addition to the professional specialist diploma was granted a one year salary increase at their new rank.

Chapter 12

FROM COWRIES TO CURRENCY

When I was a child, the money widely used was the cowry, a sea shell. Alongside this was the money introduced by the Colonial Administration. In the early 1930's, a school child had a satisfying meal by eating a five-cowry worth of akara ball before going to school in the mornings; in those days, the akara ball was heavy and nutritious (akara is made from ground soaked beans to which was added salt, pepper, and other flavoured spices or condiments, mixed thoroughly in a bowl and then fried as balls from a dessert spoonful). A few decades later, it had become the fashion in making akara to grind the beans after having removed the outer skin, making it easier to blow up the ground mixture to aerate it before frying; this process made the akara much lighter and tastier, but less satisfying to the hungry man. With this development, akara was no longer the poor and average man's food, and it cost a lot more, helping to phase out the cowry rapidly. I learnt quite early that the cowry system was being phased out by the government.

In the districts in which I grew up, and also in many parts of Nigeria in those days, there was also significant trade by barter. I experienced this when I entered secondary school in 1941. A student who desired to acquire a wrist watch or a fountain pen would exchange a shirt or two, or a pair of shorts with the trader, according to the value of the commodity. Other students found it much fun if and when such a wrist watch stopped working after a week or two and the owner would bang his wrist on the desk from time to time in the hope of restarting the watch !

The government coins had local names. A half-penny was called 'hey peennie';,one penny was called 'kobo'; the three penny bit was known as 'taw-raw' the six pence coin was called 'sisi' and the shilling (equivalent to twelve pence) was known as 'soo-lay'; later a one-tenth penny piece popularly called '***ah-nee-nee***' was introduced. Higher value denominations were paper money of ten shillings, and a pound (a pound was twenty shillings). The one-guinea, valued one pound & one shilling, that was in use in Britain did not get reflected in Nigerian currency, neither in market transactions nor in business documents. The exchange rate for cowries was twenty cowries to one penny, and Nigerian currency was at par with the currency in the United Kingdom well into the sixties. As might be expected, with two types of currency in circulation ***money changers*** made good profit from exchanging paper money for coins, and coins for cowries and vice-versa. The paper money as well as the coins were embossed British West Africa and so were valid for use in all the British West African Colonies.

Nigerians persisted in calling pennies "kobo" long after independence and so it was that on January 1, 1973, when Gowon's Military Administration r introduced the new decimal currency, they named it Naira and Kobo, with one hundred Kobo being equal to a Naira. Appropriate coins and notes (paper money) of different values were introduced. These were modified in a few years, and by 1999 to 2000, new value notes were introduced. Most unfortunately, these modifications coincided with significant devaluation which has continued till today, two decades into the new millennium ! In 1973, the naira was rated at par with the British Ten shillings (or two naira to the pound), and therefore valued more than a U S dollar. Currently, the naira is fluctuating between 450 and 600 to the pound while the relationship with the U S dollar ranges between 350 and 450. The unfortunate consequence of this trend is that all coins of the Nigerian currency of value two naira, one naira and all grades of kobo have unavoidably disappeared from usage and circulation, and all Nigerians below the age of twenty years have not seen and may never see them except in the museums. This exit will further broaden the era of ***forgotten days.***

EPILOGUE

GOD IS IN CONTROL

Baba and Mama decided to make a clean break from the traditional way of life in the environment into which they were born. The basis was religious belief and this sustained them throughout their lives. Many people have often wondered how their own lives have played out, with unexpected events, trials and tribulations, encounters in the progress of life, and meeting, quite casually, persons who eventually played key roles in their lives. Some call it good luck if all goes well and bad luck if the trend of life goes against all expectations. Another view is, like most pure scientists, to say that how we live is generally determined by our DNA and the environment. Evolution is an explanation that seems acceptable to many other enquiring minds. My view based on my life experiences is very simply that **"God is in control, all the time"**, just as my parents taught me.

One of my classmates in GCI had wanted to study medicine like me, but his "family" told him quite bluntly that their preference was law because theirs was about the only family in the community that had no lawyer; consequently their family was looked down upon and he complied reluctantly. He turned out to be a successful lawyer, later rising in rank to become a Judge.

E F Smith became my teacher at Igarra (KCSG) in 1939 during the period of short-term staff appointments, and later went to train as a priest of the CMS Church. Later still as a fully trained priest, he served as Pastor in charge of St James's Church in Benin City, the church my sister Mama Benin attended regularly. Consequently, Reverend Smith played a significant role in my life.

From the late 1890's when Baba my father became a Christian, he had absolute confidence and trust in God and this enabled him to live happily in spite of all odds. In the various communities in which he served as Catechist, he often received donations of crops at harvest time from church members who were farmers, and some gave Baba portions of their farmland for Baba to use and develop to his taste. All this augmented his meagre salary as Catechist, but the hand of God was evident in his life all the time. My secondary education on government scholarship, followed by post-secondary and university training leading to my becoming a medical doctor, at government expense confirms God's blessing on him.

As referred to in the sub-heading **Preparation for post-primary education in chapter 6**, my father's hope and aspiration for Edward Albert and me was that we should become university graduates. He and Mama believed and trusted in God that it would happen; Mama would always sigh and say **How can we finance it all,** and Baba would follow by saying **Leave it in God's hands.** Edward did obtain a bachelor's degree from University of Nigeria, Nsukka followed by a post-graduate teacher's diploma at Leeds University in the United Kingdom; Albert had his basic degree from Cornell University, New York in United States of America, followed by post-graduate and doctoral studies in Sociology & Anthropology in Universities in Uppsala Sweden, Ibadan and Lagos in Nigeria; I graduated with bachelor degrees in medicine & surgery from University of London, followed by post-graduate studies in Royal College of Surgeons, London and University of Liverpool, England. Baba lived to just over a hundred years, and realised his hopes, **God is in control.**

Following my housemanship appointments in different hospitals in England, I found myself guided into the specialty of Orthopaedic Surgery commencing at the Bath & Wessex Orthopaedic Hospital, a specialty which I continued to practise when I returned to Nigeria, and indeed, all my working years. A short spell of General Practice immediately after I retired from Government service in 1975, while it was financially very attractive and lucrative, was not professionally satisfying; that was when, with the understanding and support of my wife and family, I returned to organised systematic orthopaedic practice in a University & Teaching Hospital in Benin City.

Years rolled by, and in the year 2015, Claris and I celebrated our 60th wedding anniversary. On that occasion she reminded me that we had had so many different experiences over the past sixty years and more, and that but for God, our life story would have been different; putting it down in writing in the hope of getting it published, might not only be interesting reading to many people but may be helpful too, especially to young couples who may be anxious about what the future holds for them. ***"Why don't we try? People must always remember that God is in control, all the time"*** she said. That is the background that has inspired the production of this book, by faith in divine guidance and control.

About the Author

Professor F A Orhewere is an orthopaedic surgeon whose passion for his work led to a career of outstanding service to his home country Nigeria, and the love and respect of colleagues and co-workers, students, patients and their relatives. Born into a humble family, he had his basic education in Nigeria, was a foundation student of the University of Ibadan, and was sent to the UK to complete his medical studies. He returned to Nigeria, and worked for many years at the National Orthopaedic Hospital in Lagos, Later, he joined the University of Benin, becoming Dean of the School of Medicine and the Deputy Vice-Chancellor. The latter part of his career was dedicated to training doctors and providing professional expertise in Sokoto state, Northern Nigeria, continuing to work there after it was divided into Sokoto, Kebbi and Zamfara States. He remained the only orthopaedic surgeon in the huge area covered by those three states for nearly a decade. He has inspired many young people and is a natural story-teller.

CW01263160

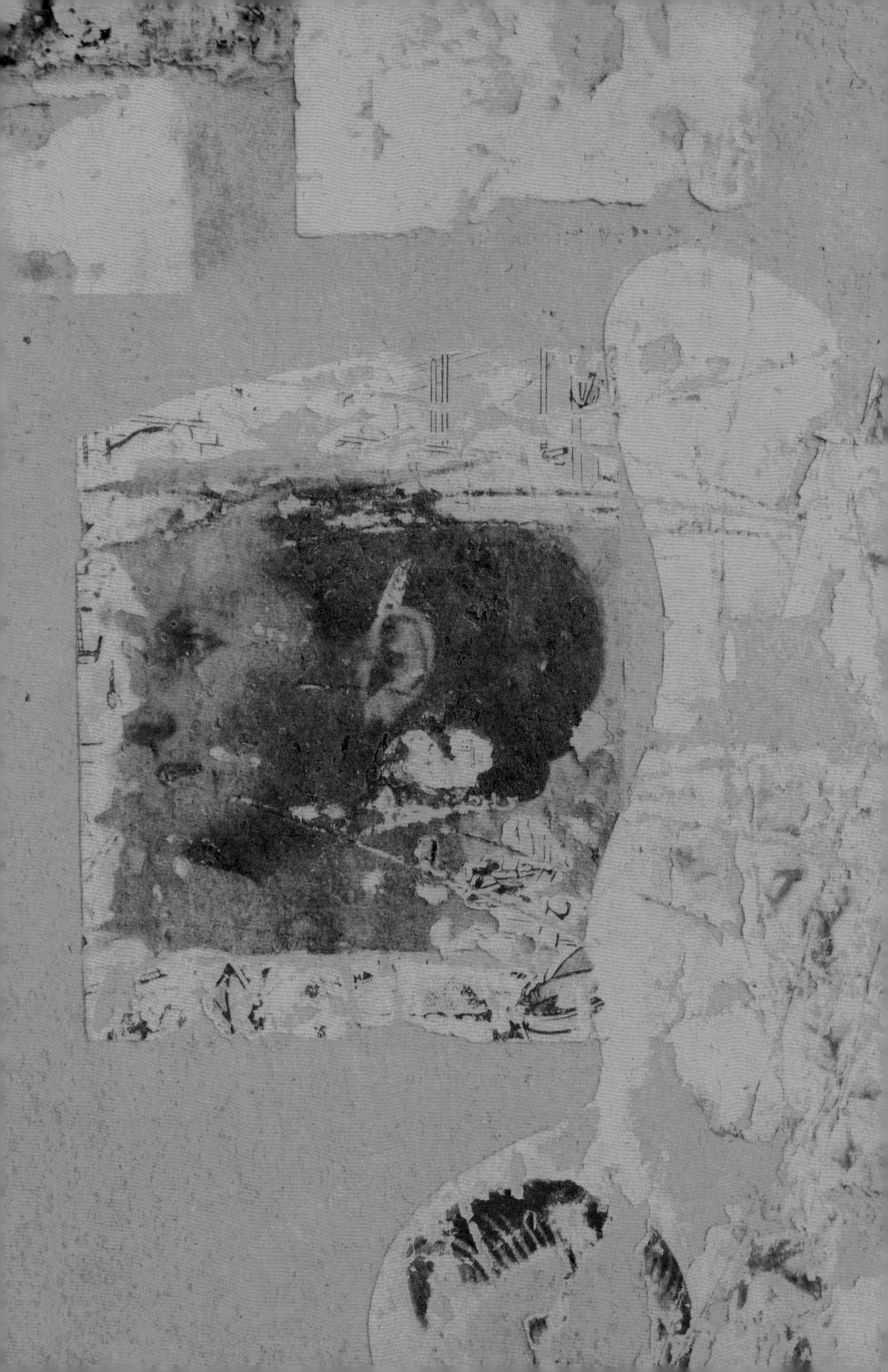

Published by Turning Point Books
15th floor, Concorde Building, Dunan Street
Verdun, Beirut, Lebanon
P.O. Box: 14-6613
Tel: +961 1 752 100
www.tpbooksonline.com
First edition: June 2012
Text: Shirine Saad
Editing: Joanne Sayad
Photos: Tanya Traboulsi
Graphic Design & Art Direction: Laurent el Khoury

Text Copyright © Shirine Saad, 2012
Photos Copyright © Tanya Traboulsi, 2012
Graphic Design Copyright © Turning Point Books, 2012

All rights reserved.
No part of this publication may be produced or transmitted in any form or any means without the permission of the publisher.
ISBN 978-9953-0-2388-5
Printing: Dots | www.53dots.com
While every effort has been made to ensure the accuracy of the information within this guidebook, the author and publisher accept no responsibility for any modifications, omissions or errors regarding the information contained herein.

BOHO BEIRUT

ABOUT THE AUTHOR

Shirine Saad has lived in France, Canada, Lebanon and the U.S. She studied art history and international development and holds an M.A. in arts journalism from the Columbia School of Journalism. After working as a lifestyle editor in Montreal, Saad moved to Brooklyn, where she covers art, fashion, travel and food. Her work has been published in *The New York Times, MTV, Jalouse, Aïshti, L'Officiel Levant* and *En Route*. When not sampling reindeer tongue in Helsinki, skiing in Colorado or roaming the museums of St. Petersburg, Saad travels between Beirut and Brooklyn.

BOHO BEIRUT

ACKNOWLEDGEMENTS

I would like to thank my publisher, Charlotte Hamaoui, for believing in this project and allowing the team to stay true to its creative vision. Without my editor Joanne Sayad's patience, knowledge and support, this book would not be finished today. My family has proved to be a great team of reporters, sampling food at restaurants, visiting boutiques, offering insights and – as always – providing emotional support. A huge thanks to Marwan Naaman for his continuous encouragement. Olivier Gasnier Duparc, the most Lebanese French expat I know, gave me precious insider tips and contact information. My friend Tim Murphy, a journalist, always has the right advice; he helped me find the title for this book. Last but not least, the book's creative team - graphic designer Laurent el Khoury and photographer Tanya Traboulsi - has done beautiful and original work.

BOHO BEIRUT

To my family

-١٢-

TABLE OF CONTENTS

15 PREFACE

THE NEIGHBORHOODS OF BEIRUT 16

22 ART/CULTURE

ARCHITECTURE/DESIGN 46

68 EAT

92 ~~DRINK~~

SHOP 112

STAY/TIPS 136

156 SUMMER ESCAPE

THINGS TO KNOW 160

162 MAP

A GUIDE TO THE MIDDLE EAST'S MOST SOPHISTICATED CITY

PREFACE

Many Lebanese born during the civil war, which ravaged the country for fifteen years, have lived most of their lives scattered throughout the world. For all those years we have tried to find meaning in our aimless wandering, looking back to our homeland seeking clues and answers. Sadly, many of my friends in New York or Paris still view Beirut solely through the prism of war. But Lebanon is also a bounty of nature, of sun, of infinite seas and mountains, a lively country with a generous and warm people-a land with 5,000 years of history, where great civilizations have left their traces. People of different religions and ethnicities have coexisted in this tiny land for centuries; the real Beirutis are resilient, open, tolerant and joyful. To me, as to many of us, Beirut also represents freedom and hope.

I have so much admiration for those who moved back to Beirut after the civil war – artists, musicians, chefs, architects, curators and others, full of hope and confusion, determined to make a mark in a shattered country that gives so much pain and yet that is one in which they continue to believe. Despite the wars and assassinations, the censorship and corruption, they continue to fight with ideas and art. Defying the lack of public or private funding and cultural institutions, they create events that bring people together-rethinking the legacy of the war while everyone else has erased its memories. In the absence of corporate or government sponsorship, a genuine underground culture has blossomed. Once again, and in spite of the regional turmoil, Beirut is a dynamic cultural capital.

This book pays homage to these courageous and creative Beirutis, to their determination, courage and vision. Seeking out Beirut's new tastemakers, I have interviewed up-and-coming art entrepreneurs, chefs, designers, hoteliers and night owls; threaded throughout their musings, Beirut's new face shines through.

And for those eager to discover this epicurean city's choicest offerings, I share my address book, filled with charming boutiques, delicious restaurants, posh bars and gritty clubs. I ask friends for insider tips: what to order at restaurants, which rooftop pool is the coolest, where to purchase elegant gifts and where to head for the best contemporary art exhibitions. Expect to laze around during the day, walking around Beirut's quaint streets or gazing at the Mediterranean; at night, the city wakes up and parties until sunrise. Indeed, some clichés are right: Beirut is a decadent city, buzzing with energy and always inviting people for one more night of sleepless fun.

But, Beirut also defies all clichés: It is a city of chaos and peace, of uncertainty and celebration, of innovation and deep history. We love its contradictions and complexity. We hope you do, too.

SHIRINE SAAD

THE NEIGHBORHOODS *OF* BEIRUT

BOHO BEIRUT

Ashrafieh/Gemmayze

What used to be the charming home of Beirut's aristocracy and artisan workshops is now the buzzing heart of Beirut's nightlife scene. Along the main strip of Gemmayze are more than a hundred bars and restaurants; every night the streets are filled with intoxicated tourists and locals hopping from bar to bar. Along the way, the legendary St. Nicolas yellow stone stairway is a hotspot for lovers and artists. Not too far along Sursock Street the Nicolas Sursock Museum, a beautiful example of traditional Lebanese palaces, is redesigning its exhibition space.

Beirut Souks

If the charms of Beirut's old markets (where people of all backgrounds once gathered to purchase jewelry, flowers and clothes) have vanished, post-war Solidere has renovated historic buildings and created an upscale shopping district designed by Pritzker Prize-winning Rafael Moneo. Today's Beirut Souks are filled with luxury boutiques, from Chloé to Rolex and elegant cafés and restaurants.

THE NEIGHBORHOODS OF **BEIRUT**

*Corniche

The Corniche is one of the last free leisure spaces in Beirut. Snaking along the sea, the promenade is where couples meet for dates, people of all ages jog and families picnic. Along the way you'll find vendors selling coffee, *ka'ak*, a local sesame bread, or even counterfeit perfumes.

*Hamra

Hamra is often referred to as the real Beirut: Its tiny streets are dotted with kitsch vendors, street food stalls, theaters and old coffee shops. Before the civil war Hamra Street was known as the city's Champs Elysées, as tourists would flock in to shop or to watch Egyptian romances at the Picadilly Theater. It was also an important regional intellectual center: Poets, writers and students from the area's universities discussed Arab nationalism and Umm Kulthum in its coffee shops. Now young people are moving in and opening bars, cultural venues and coffee shops again, bringing new energy to the area.

Jisr el Wati

Along the often dried out Beirut River, Jisr el Wati, an industrial area at the outskirts of the city, has become Beirut's new DumBo. With the opening of the Beirut Art Center, Homeworks, the Art Lounge and the launch of architect-designed loft developments, the graffiti-covered walls of this once sinister neighborhood are now home to a bustling creative activity.

Karantina

The ghosts of Karantina, a former refugee camp and the site of many horrors and massive factories, are finally waning. The area is bustling with art galleries, architects' studios and design lofts.

*Mar Mikhael

Further down past Gemmayze, towards the outskirts of the city, Mar Mikhael's gritty auto repair shops and hardware store-filled streets are now assailed with independent bookstores, artsy bars, organic restaurants and cutting-edge galleries.

*Saifi Village

This cluster of traditional townhouses and narrow cobblestone streets has been completely restored and painted in bright pink, yellow and orange tones. The area is filled with pretty designer boutiques and luxury apartments. On the central square, near the sculpture and fountain, is Balima Café, one of the city's hottest meeting spots, where groups gather to smoke, drink coffee and munch on sophisticated salads on the outdoor tables, and of course to engage in people watching and gossip, two favorite national sports.

BOHO BEIRUT

*SoPo

Right across from the city's major commercial port, one tiny street has been adopted by high-end retailers: IF, couturier Rabih Kayrouz and designer Karen Chekerdjian. Lux, a laid-back brasserie serving farm-to-table dishes, is just around the corner.

*Zaitunay Bay

Where sailors once docked to seek drinks and girls, a sleek new promenade designed by starchitect Steven Holl now offers champagne, lobster rolls and hummus espuma. After years of development, the new Zaitunay Bay is a peaceful spot to have a drink at sunset, perhaps after a day of yachting or water sports at the Water Nation Sports Center or design shopping at Nada Debs. If you're feeling more nautical, St Elmo's brasserie serves seaside treats – oysters and lobster galore, ice-cold beer and fun cocktails.

A&C
ART/CULTURE

The Lebanese civil war annihilated most cultural activities for more than fifteen years, paralyzing institutions and sending many artists into exile. Until today the government is in constant crisis and struggles to sustain social or cultural programs. Artists and organizers, many of whom returned to Lebanon in the post-war years with the dream of contributing to their country's new cultural dialogue, are left to their own means. Yet their passion and determination have created a unique and vibrant artistic environment. In the nineties, indie bands started experimenting with different traditions, mixing traditional Arabic music with other genres such as pop, hip-hop and post-punk. Poets, dancers, actors and filmmakers, mostly unhindered by censorship, explore the legacy of Lebanon's chaotic history, trying to make sense of the absurdity and violence that the country still witnesses. As the Middle East's art market started to soar in the 2000s, a slew of world-class galleries opened in the city, representing the best talent from the region. Foreign artists, lured by this creative energy, are moving into the city, bringing their own traditions and skills into the mix. In this inspiring environment, artistic exchanges and intellectual debates are helping the Lebanese to rethink their country's changing identity – neither mimicking Western artists nor falling into the trappings of Orientalist nostalgia.

A GUIDE TO THE MIDDLE EAST'S MOST SOPHISTICATED CITY

01 *Agial

Saleh Barakat is one of Lebanon's leading art experts who has helped build important art collections and curated several influential exhibitions, including at the Venice Biennial. In 1991 Barakat opened his own gallery, Agial, focusing on regional painters including the very successful Paul Guiragossian and Ayman Baalbaki. Since then the gallerist has been nominated as a Yale fellow and as the head of a new museum project at the American University of Beirut.

Tip: Agial has an impressive permanent collection that includes paintings by leading local artists.
- Address: Abdul Aziz Street, Hamra
- Tel. 01- 345 213 / 03-634 244
- W.agialart.com

02 *ArtFactum

Joy Mardini has studied art history and worked at auction houses, including Christie's and Tajan, in Paris. Back in Beirut she managed the Kettaneh-Kunig gallery, a world reference, and also worked with their Munich sister space. Now Mardini has her own space, ArtFactum, a state-of-the-art two floor industrial gallery in a former Quarantina wrought iron factory. There, she exhibits contemporary art from across the world. From Lebanon's Tanya Traboulsi's photographs of her country to Spain's Dario Basso's abstract paintings and Mustapha Azeroual's black-and-white images, Mardini's selection is sharp and diverse.

Tip: ArtFactum has a beautiful selection of art books for sale.
- Address: Rehban Street, Karantina
- Tel. 01-443 263
- W.Artfactumgallery.com

03 *Ashkal Alwan/Homeworks*

The Ashkal Alwan association is a strong promoter of local art. It also organizes Homeworks, a multidisciplinary platform that brings together artists and thinkers from all over the world every other year. They are asked to reflect on urgent social, political or artistic issues through workshops, events and forums. Now the association has opened a contemporary art center and academy. There, in a raw concrete space designed by architect Youssef Tohme, a multimedia research library, artist studios, an exhibition space, performance spaces and academic programs allow local and international artists to perfect their skills, collaborate and show their work.

Tip: Christine Tohme, the director of the association, is a prestigious curator and expert on Arab art. Consult her if you're interested in collecting.
- Address: 90 Street, Jisr el Wati
- Tel. 01-423 879
- W.ashkalwan.com

04 *Ayyam*

Founded in Damascus in 2006, Ayyam Gallery is one of the most prestigious galleries in the Middle East and now has branches in Beirut, Dubai and Geneva. Iraqi artist Sadik Alfraji's powerfully graphic mixed-media works and Damascene artist Assad Arabi's bright, expressionistic nude paintings are particularly interesting. The gallery has supported regional art through several initiatives, including The Shabab Ayyam Project, an incubator program for young artists and Ayyam Auctions, which hosts biannual public sales.

Tip: Sign up to the gallery's mailing list; you will be invited to Ayyam's cocktail parties, where guests mingle on Platinum Tower's terrace drinking champagne.
- Address: Beirut Tower, Zaitunay Street
- Tel. 01-374 450
- W.ayyamgallery.com

05 *BAC

This former factory in the industrial Jisr el Wati area has been transformed into a cool 1,500 square meter contemporary art museum. Sandra Dagher and Lamia Joreige, the directors, created the Beirut Art Center in 2010 to promote local and international art and give local visitors access to cutting-edge cultural activities. The non-profit association has exhibited the work of Palestinian conceptual artist Mouna Hatoum, multimedia artist Chris Marker, painter Gerhard Richter and Lebanese writer and artist Walid Sadek; the BAC also organizes a series of avant-garde music performances in its auditorium every Wednesday night.

Tip: Stop by BAC Design on the second floor, which often features emerging designers whose work can be purchased. Also look out for the opening of the roof-terrace.
- Address: 97 Street, Jisr el Wati
- Tel. 01-397 018
- W.beirutartcenter.org

06 *Beirut Exhibition Center

In a city that suffers from the lack of a major art museum, the new Beirut Exhibition Center is a great new space for large-scale exhibitions. It showcases local and regional art in a dramatic setting designed by experimental Lebanese architecture firm L.E.F.T. With its faceted, wavelike mirrored skin, the building reflects the surrounding sea and sky, standing out in this city of concrete. Inside, a vast gallery hosts important collective exhibitions such as the Sursock Museum's *Salon d'Automne* and retrospectives of conceptual artists Johanna Hadjithomas and Khalil Joreige and painter Shafic Abboud. There is also a cozy café and adjacent garden for leisurely summer afternoons.

Tip: The BEC also organizes workshops for children with a focus on local art history.
- Address: Beirut New Waterfront
- Tel. 01-962 000 ext. 2883
- W.beirutexhibitioncenter.com

07 *Beirut National Museum

Over 1,300 archeological artifacts dating from Prehistoric to Ottoman times are exhibited at the Beirut National Museum, bearing witness to the deep history of the Levant. This collection was first established by a French colonial officer in 1919 and the museum was inaugurated in 1937. After the civil war had destroyed much of its structure, it underwent substantial repairs and is now fully restored. Marvels include a Venus statue from the Hellenistic period, a Roman sarcophagus from Tyre, gold and pearl Byzantine jewels, and patterned ceramics from the Mamluke era.

Tip: At the Museum store, you will find a stellar selection of books about the region's history and archaeology.
- Address: Mathaf, Beirut
- Tel. 01-426 703 (4)
- W.beirutnationalmuseum.com

08 *Janine Rubeiz

Janine Rubeiz founded "Dar el Fan," Lebanon's first cultural center, in 1967, but it was destroyed in 1975 at the beginning of the civil war. Still, Rubeiz pursued her artistic activities in her own apartment throughout the crises, convinced that a vibrant cultural dialogue was essential to the country's sanity. Her daughter, Nadine Bekdache, took over in 1990, perpetuating her mother's mission. She transformed the apartment into a gallery to exhibit works by artists from around the world, including Moebius and the painter and poet Etel Adnan. Today the gallery maintains a notable presence at art fairs and auction houses, continuing to influence and nourish the local art scene.

Tip: Nadine Bekdache's son, Karim, is one of the country's leading architects.
- Address: Charles Malek Avenue, Raouche
- Tel. 01-868 290
- W.galeriejaninerubeiz.com

09 *Kettaneh-Kunig

Photography and installation from the Middle East is the highlight of this West Beirut gallery owned by Naila Kettaneh-Kunig. She represents established local talent such as Fouad el Khoury and Lamia Joreige as well as emerging artists such as Zena al Khalil, whose large multicolored collages parody the region's politics. The gallery also exhibits international art stars such as Jeff Koons, Sylvie Fleury and Marc Quinn, who were featured in the Luxury and Degradation show.

Tip: Fouad el Khoury is a leading photographer in the country; his black and white photographs of Beirut are beautiful and poetic.
- Address: Gefinor Center, Clemenceau
- Tel. 01-738 706
- W.galerietanit.com

10 *Lebanese Film Festival

Most foreigners are familiar with the legendary West Beirut (1998) and Caramel (2007), but many of the best Lebanese films rarely make it abroad. The Lebanese Film Festival, launched by a group of young film lovers a decade ago, showcases the best of local production and international films made about the country every year. From shorts to feature films and documentaries, the event is a window on the creativity and depth of the country's artistic scene. The festival also supports local filmmakers and helps them thrive at festivals abroad.

Tip: The Festival compilations showcase the best Lebanese films of the past decade.

11 *Metropolis Cinema

There was a time when most new art house releases could not be found in Lebanese theaters and film lovers had scarce alternatives to Hollywood blockbusters. But since 2006, the Lebanese Association for Art House Cinemas, Metropolis, regularly features the world's best auteur films. The space also hosts Arab film festivals, special screenings and talks, contributing to the dynamic Arab film scene.

Tip: Hania Mroue, the founder of Metropolis, was a juror at the 2012 Berlinale and promotes Arabic cinema throughout Europe. Ask her for a list of DVDs to take home.
- Address: Sofil Center, Ashrafieh
- Tel. 01-332 661
- W.metropolis.info

12 *Plan Bey

This tiny concept store in Mar Mikhael is filled with art books, postcards of local photographers' work, gift items and a stellar selection of jazz and classical music CDs. The owner, Tony Sfeir, who managed music store and production house CDthèque for years, handpicks every single object on display, including artworks by local artists. He also organizes exhibitions and cultural events.

Tip: Pick up a glass jar with a candle by Alexandra Wardé, covered in nostalgic images of Lebanon.
- Address: Armenia Street, Mar Mikhael
- Tel. 01-444 110
- W.plan-bey.com

13 *Q Gallery

This new art space on the ground floor of the luxurious Beirut Tower is vast, flooded with light and filled with world-class contemporary artworks. There, a team of curators organizes exhibitions of Arab and international art every month; Syrian owner Motaz Kabbani's private collection, which mainly focuses on Arab art, is also on display (and on sale). Featured artists include Lebanese painter and print artist Mohamed Rawas, whose installation *Sit Down Please* mixes calligraphy, dolls, silkscreens and a video where actors recite words from poet Abu Nawas in sign language. Q is the partner of Ayyam, the gallery next door.

Tip: Q is a few steps away from the Zaitunay Bay promenade, where you can contemplate the Mediterranean horizon and luxury yachts anchored in the marina.

- Address: Beirut Tower, Zaitunay Street, Downtown
- Tel. 03-300 520
- W.qcontemporary.com

14 *Sfeir-Semler

In the Karantina area, gallerist Andrée Sfeir-Semler has taken over an industrial space. When Sfeir-Semler, who also owns a gallery in Hamburg, discovered conceptual media artist Walid Raad and his fictional collective the Atlas Project, she realized a brilliant art scene was emerging in the region. In 2008 she invited Catherine David, previously curator at the Centre Georges Pompidou and the Jeu de Paume and director of the Documenta X, to organize a thematic exhibition. For the show In the Middle of the Middle, David asked twelve artists from multinational backgrounds to portray their cultural realities. Sfeir-Semler sells works to MoMA, the Tate Modern and the Saatchi Gallery in London, which has included several of her artists in the exhibition Unveiled: New Art from the Middle-East.

Tip: Two of the gallery's younger multimedia artists, Mounira el Solh and Rayyane Tabet, were featured in the New Museum's Ungovernables triennial.

- Address: 56 Street, Karantina
- Tel. 01-566 550
- W.sfeir-semler.com

15 *The Running Horse

After graduating from Central Saint Martins in 2008, Lea Sednaoui initially planned to convert a former mattress depot into a personal sculpture studio. Changing her mind, she chose to open a gallery instead. Some of Sednaoui's most successful artists are Alfred Tarazi, whose provocative prints are particularly popular, and Rasha Kahil, whose witty, sharp photographs are at once satirical and poetic. Sednaoui particularly likes to create thematic group shows such as Counting Thoughts, where nine female artists from around the world were invited to express their interpretation of womanhood.

Tip: Lea is an expert on cultural activities in Beirut. Ask her for a list of things to do.
- Address: Shukri Al Khoury Street, Karantina
- Tel. 01-562 778
- W.therunninghorseart.com

16 *Zico House

In a beautiful old Lebanese house near the Sanayeh Park, Zico House is one of the city's coolest cultural centers, hosting street theater festivals, contemporary dance shows and art exhibitions. Named after its owner, Mohammed "Zico" Yammout, the house also hosts international artists for workshops and residences. Try Firas Yatbokh ("Firas cooks") for vegetarian dinners and music or come to one of the summer dance parties and mingle in the luxuriant backyard garden.

Tip: If you're looking for a reasonably priced room during your trip, Zico can accommodate you – just mention my name.
- Address: Spears Street, Sanayeh
- Tel. 01-746 769
- W.zicohouse.org

Mashrouh Leila

Scrambled Eggs

BOHO BEIRUT

BEIRUT'S OWN BANDS

Beirut's indie music scene is more lively than ever. Inspired by their travels and exchanges, musicians draw on their multicultural heritage to create unique and powerful sounds. If you want to check out a few concerts or purchase some CDs, here are some names to remember. Scrambled Eggs is a veteran on the local rock scene; its raw, rebellious sound is reminiscent of the post-punk scenes of Seattle or Manchester. Zeid Hamdan is a legend on the local music scene; his Arabic trip-hop band Soap Kills established a new sound in the nineties. Now Hamdan is at the helm of Beirut Music Underground, a group that brings together the city's best bands. He also plays his softly melancholic music with his band, Zeid and the Wings. Mashrouh Leila is one of the best new bands in town; their original, contemporary Arabic songs are a must-hear. The Beirut hip-hop scene is thriving and is very influential in the Arab world: Three names to seek out are El Rass, Fareeq el Atrash and Malikah.

THE TASTEMAKERS

SANDRA DAGHER
THE ART PATRON

HOW DOES BEIRUT INSPIRE YOU?

{ BEIRUT IS AN ATYPICAL CITY FULL OF SURPRISES AND UNEXPECTED DISCOVERIES. BUT MORE THAN A SOURCE OF INSPIRATION, IT IS A SOURCE FOR OPPORTUNITIES AND GIVES YOU THE CHANCE TO DEVELOP NEW PROJECTS. }

BOHO BEIRUT

- 35 -

A GUIDE TO THE MIDDLE EAST'S MOST SOPHISTICATED CITY

THE TASTEMAKERS:

SANDRA DAGHER
The art patron

Sandra Dagher fled war-torn Beirut with her family, grew up in Paris and moved back to her hometown after studies in photography. In 2000 she inaugurated Espace SD, a massive cultural space in the then dormant Mar Mikhael area. She organized exhibitions, concerts and film screenings and played an important role in bringing together young artists, helping to build a new cutting-edge cultural scene. Dagher also handpicked artists for the Lebanese pavilion at the Venice Biennial for several years. After closing her first space in 2007, she teamed up with multimedia artist Lamia Joreige to open the Beirut Art Center, the most ambitious contemporary art center in the country, in the industrial Jisr el Wati area. With the help of architect Raed Abillama, an abandoned factory was transformed into a vast concrete two-floor center that hosts exhibitions of works of leading artists from the region and the rest of the world. The center's auditorium also hosts contemporary performances; during events guests mingle on the center's raw concrete terrace.

ARTISTS TO WATCH?
There are many interesting established and emerging artists in Lebanon. To name a few: Akram Zaatari, Paola Yacoub, Fouad el Khoury, Rabih Mroué, Nadim Asfar, and Raed Yassin.

FAVORITE BAR?
I enjoy going to Behind the Green Door for an early drink. The music is nice and the atmosphere is warm and comfortable.

BEST RESTAURANT?
My favorite restaurant is Casablanca. But I also like The Gathering, three small restaurants in old Lebanese houses with a central courtyard.

BEST ART SPACES?
The most interesting galleries in the city are Agial and Sfeir-Semler. Art Factum, also looks very promising.

A GUIDE TO THE MIDDLE EAST'S MOST SOPHISTICATED CITY

BEHIND THE GREEN DOOR
PORT VIEW BUILDING, MAR MIKHAEL
TEL. 01-565 656
CASABLANCA
DAR EL-MREISSEH STREET, AIN EL-MREISSEH
TEL. 01-369 334
THE GATHERING
PASTEUR STREET, GEMMAYZE
TEL. 01-566 196
AGIAL
63 ABDUL AZIZ STREET, HAMRA
TEL. 01-345 213 / 03-634 244
SFEIR-SEMLER
TANNOUS BUILDING, KARANTINA
TEL. 01-566 550
ART FACTUM
KARANTINA
TEL. 01-443 263

BOHO BEIRUT

ADDRESS BOOK

SANDRA DAGHER

A GUIDE TO THE MIDDLE EAST'S MOST SOPHISTICATED CITY

A&C

THE TASTEMAKERS

SHARIF SEHNAOUI
THE IMPROVISATOR

HOW DOES BEIRUT INSPIRE YOU?

{ CERTAIN THINGS ABOUT THE CITY SOMETIMES BOTHER ME AND CERTAIN THINGS ARE INHUMANE, BUT I THINK THERE'S A TRUE RICHNESS TO THIS COUNTRY AND A VERY STRONG IDENTITY. A FRAGMENTED, MULTIPLE IDENTITY. }

BOHO BEIRUT

-41-

Dans les Arbres concert

A GUIDE TO THE MIDDLE EAST'S MOST SOPHISTICATED CITY

A&C

THE TASTEMAKERS:

SHARIF SEHNAOUI
The improvisator

Sharif Sehnaoui discovered jazz as a music student in Paris. He listened to Ornette Coleman, John Coltrane, Cecil Taylor and Evan Parker and studied the Paris jazz scene of the sixties. As Sehnaoui strove to develop his own musical identity, he migrated towards free jazz, creating spontaneous and complex sounds on his guitar. When he moved back to Lebanon, Sehnaoui discovered a pulsating music scene and started playing concerts with his friends. In 2001 he created Irtijal, an avant-garde music festival featuring local and international artists, with musician Mazen Kerbaj (*irtijal* means improvisation). Post-rock, jazz, electronic music, free improvisation: the festival welcomes all genres. The only rule is true innovation and experimentation. When not planning and negotiating Sehnaoui plays in several Beirut bands, including Scrambled Eggs and Friends, Bao, A trio and Oriental Space. He and his partners have also just inaugurated a cultural center, Yukunkun, in a Gemmayze basement, where they host concerts, performances and parties.

FAVORITE ART SPACE?
I organize cultural events every Wednesday at the Beirut Art Center's auditorium. The entire experimental Lebanese music scene has performed there -- including Scrambled Eggs, Fadi Tabbal and Tarek Atoui.

BEST PLACE TO PURCHASE CDS?
Chico DVD in Hamra has excellent CDs from local labels.

BEST THEATER?
I like Masrah el Madina, an exceptional theater. There's a large room for major productions -including the Maqamat dance festival-and a small concert space and cabaret.

BEST BAR?
DRM in Hamra has a high-quality music program and performances.

BOHO BEIRUT

A GUIDE TO THE MIDDLE EAST'S MOST SOPHISTICATED CITY

A&C

BEIRUT ART CENTER (BAC)
BUILDING 13, STREET 97, ZONE 66 ADLIEH, JISR EL WATI
TEL. 01-397 018
CHICO DVD
SIDANI STREET, HAMRA
TEL. 01-743 855
MASRAH AL-MADINA
SAROULLA BUILDING, HAMRA STREET
TEL. 01-753 010/11
MAQAMAT DANCE THEATRE
ISPRAL CENTER, HAMRA STREET
TEL. 01-343 834
DRM
SOURATI BUILDING, SOURATI STREET, HAMRA
TEL. 01-752 202

~~ADDRESS~~ BOOK

SHARIF SEHNAOUI

A GUIDE TO THE MIDDLE EAST'S MOST SOPHISTICATED CITY

A&C

A&D

ARCHITECTURE/DESIGN

Beirut is often described as an ugly and beautiful city, a study in contrasts. The shoreline, increasingly exploited by private developers, has been artificially altered. Concrete towers rise chaotically, many of them left unfinished, competing for sea views. The civil war annihilated many of the city's public spaces and landmarks, leaving several scarred buildings. While many of the city's old houses are crumbling or being replaced by high rises, Solidere, the company for the development of the city center, has revived the old souks, restoring several traditional Ottoman houses. Sadly, its high-end boutiques and soaring real estate prices prevent Lebanese of all classes from mingling freely, as they did at the old markets. But explore Beirut's narrow streets and you'll find stone houses with red-tiled roofs and arcade windows, colorful gardens on cast iron balconies and striking modernist buildings mixing steel and concrete. This is Beirut: Roman columns, Umayyad mosques, historic cathedrals and French colonial houses mingle with luxury stores, street vendors, artisans' workshops and massive construction sites. The post-civil war era, which has seen a steady influx of the generations who had come of age abroad, has allowed architects and industrial designers to thrive. Twisting traditional Lebanese objects and patterns with a contemporary touch, rethinking the country's turbulent history, today's architects and designers are creating a new Lebanese aesthetic.

A GUIDE TO THE MIDDLE EAST'S MOST SOPHISTICATED CITY

01 *Bokja

When Hoda Baroudi, an avid collector of Uzbeki and precious textiles, and Maria Hibri, an antiques dealer, started confectioning cushions with antique Uzbeki fabrics and later customized vintage furniture with patchworks of colorful Oriental textiles– Souzanis, velvets, Damascene brocade or silks, their Bokja brand was an immediate success. Now there's one Bokja chair in each Christian Louboutin store; Julia Roberts owns several pieces; Vogue editors and celebrities rave about the brand. At the boho-chic boutique in Saifi Village, each brightly hued lounger, sofa and armchair is unique and handmade by women using traditional techniques.

Tip: *"Bokja"* is a Turkish word meaning a rich fabric traditionally created to cover a bride's dowry.
- Address: Mukhallassiya Street, Saifi Village
- Tel. 01-975 576
- W.bokjadesign.com

02 *Karen Chekerdjian

Designer Karen Chekerdjian constantly questions the meaning of design and the way everyday objects shape our culture. Working with local artisans, she handcrafts contemporary objects that look back at the traditional lives of the Lebanese: "Derbakeh," a brass stool shaped like a traditional Lebanese percussion instrument; "Living Space II," a multipurpose lounger/side desk/magazine rack made of wood and traditional rattan straw; "One to two," mouth-blown glasses in the traditional turquoise color. At her SoPo boutique, Chekerdjian also sells Nathalie Khayat's porcelain objects, Tinna Gunnarsdóttir's minimalist designs and Victoria Delany's colorful "Candlestack" candles.

Tip: Karen's small brass candleholders, marked with mosaic patterns, are reasonably priced and pack easily.
- Address: Derviche Haddad Street, Beirut Port district
- Tel. 01-570 572
- W.karenchekerdjian.com

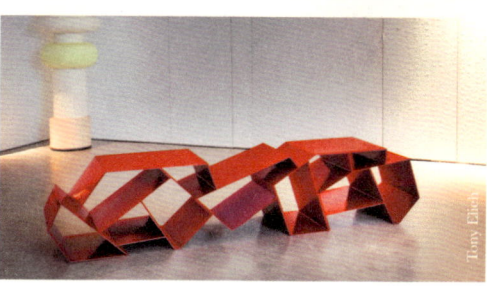

03 *Karim Bekdache

Karim Bekdache builds raw, minimalist lofts for Lebanon's artists and designers and has helped redesign the iconic Sursock Museum. He also creates stark, industrial objects with a raw finish, such as a steel office shelf with removable wooden crates and a simple concrete table. At his massive workshop on Mar Mikhael's Madrid Street, he sells his own designs alongside retro furniture and commercial signs handpicked in flea markets or off decrepit store fronts.

Tip: Karim Bekdache's mother Nadine Bekdache owns the influential Beirut gallery Janine Rubeiz. Visit it if you can.
- Address: Madrid Street, Mar Mikhael
- Tel. 01-566 323
- W.karimbekdache.com

04 *Maria Halios Design

At her Mar Mikhael showroom and design office, located in a former chocolate factory, Greek-Lebanese designer Maria Halios sells her poetic, sculptural pieces. Halios takes industrial materials such as iron and bronze and shapes them into soft flower patterns or dining tables with tree-shaped legs. She is inspired by fifties design, traveling and architecture. Halios worked as an interior designer in Paris and moved back to Lebanon a few years ago; she is one of the best designers of the new generation.

Tip: Halios also sells decorative objects handpicked on trips to Greece, such as small pomegranate ornaments.
- Address: Pharaon Street, Mar Mikhael
- Tel. 01-442 344
- W.mariahalios.com

05 *Nayef Francis

Working as a decorator for several years has helped Nayef Francis develop an insider's view on furniture and interiors. At his quaint Mar Mikhael boutique, he now offers his eponymous line, which draws on local traditions and crafts while adopting sleek forms. A faceted lamp is made of the rattan straw usually used for traditional chairs; the Turkish coffee cup is stripped of its usual ornaments and comes in neutral or brightly hued copper. The designer also creates custom pieces, reflecting the taste and needs of his clients.

Tip: Francis continues to work as an interior designer. Visit his all-white design office right across the street.
- Address: Armenia Street, Mar Mikhael
- Tel. 01-444 711
- W.nayeffrancis.com

06 *Over The Counter

The best things in life are reunited under one roof at Over the Counter, a concept store selling fine wines, contemporary design and fashion. There you will find classic Danish designs, avant-garde pieces by the British company Established & Sons and the Canadian company Molo and other companies from around the world. OTC also commissions Lebanese designers and artists to create custom items, such as the "naughty pieces" designed by musician Charbel Haber, architect Riad Kamel and photographer Joe Kesrouani.

Tip: OTC's parties are famously wild.
- Address: Abdel Wahab al-Inglizi Street, Ashrafieh
- Tel. 01-322 786
- W.over-thecounter.com

BOHO BEIRUT

07 *SMO Gallery

This stunning new gallery is owned by architect Gregory Gatserelia, known for his sleek hotel, nightclub and restaurant designs. Gatserelia is also a seasoned collector; SMO showcases unique pieces he has picked throughout the years from designers such as Ettore Sottsass, Jean Royère, Marc Newson and Andrée Putman. The gallery also sells objects by the new generation of cutting-edge Lebanese designers: a leather and steel chair by Bernard Khoury, a simple steel chair by Samer al Ameen, the mushroom-shaped Hiroshima lamp by Karen Chekerdjian and Najla el Zein's oneiric wool "Black Clouds."

Tip: Look out for the space's exhibitions and events.
- Address: 77 Sengal Street, Karantina
- Tel. 01-572 202
- W.smogallery.com

08 *XXeme Siècle

At this elegant two-story gallery, Souheil Hanna and his sister Hala sell rare vintage objects from the fifties, sixties and seventies, which they find at Paris flea markets and Christie's and Sotheby's auction sales. In the last decade they have amassed a substantial collection of Jean Royère furniture, Victor Vasarely lithographs and Oscar Niemeyer ottomans and loungers. While the general emphasis is on French, Scandinavian and Italian design, the store now also sells limited edition pieces by Lebanese designer Karen Chekerdjian.

Tip: After visiting the gallery walk around Hamra and visit the American University of Beirut's verdant campus.
- Address: Makdessi Street, Hamra
- Tel. 01-742 020
- W.xxesieclegalerie.com

BOHO BEIRUT

BERNARD KHOURY ON BEIRUT'S ARCHITECTURAL LANDSCAPE

Bernard Khoury, whose projects raise incisive questions about the country's identity, is Lebanon's most iconic architect. Khoury studied at the Rhode Island School of Design and Harvard's Architecture School and has received numerous prizes. In the nineties he became notorious for his visionary design for club B018, an underground bunker with a flat, retractable roof that struck many chords with its references to genocides, underground shelters, tombs and the Lebanese's almost morbid thirst for excess. Today Khoury designs several of the city's best residential buildings, including several industrial-inspired lofts.

"Beirut is an extremely ugly city, but it's extremely fascinating. It's full of complexities and contradictions that aren't always visible. It's a city in flux, and its identity is hard to define. While many of us in the nineties were taken with this idea of reconstructing a city, a nation, I have somehow given up on that project. In the absence of a political and historic consensus we cannot rebuild our city. There were no public projects or debates around the city or its history, including the war. History stopped with the end of the French Mandate, and now we are either importing a Western idea of modernity or creating an Orientalist fantasy for the West. However, there was a stellar architectural practice in the country during the Trente glorieuses (from the fifties to the seventies.) My favorite building from this era is my father's (architect Khalil Khoury, known as Le Corbusier of Lebanon) Interdesign project. It is a raw concrete building that represents the beginning of a modern project in the country. Like my father, I situate my practice in the present; I am looking for a specific modernity within the context of our reality and history."

NADA DEBS
A NEW DESIGN AESTHETIC

Nada Debs grew up in Japan, attended the Rhode Island School of Design, then moved to London, where she worked as a designer for several years. When she moved back to Lebanon in 2000 she realized the design scene needed more creativity. She combined the practicality of the Japanese zen aesthetic, the American "form follows function" and the British love for craftsmanship for her line East and East. Working with local craftsmen and traditions, she created a new Middle Eastern design aesthetic, inspiring several emerging designers to follow her lead. Her now world-famous creations combine ornamental Arabic patterns and colors with Zen or modernist forms. Precious wood tables are subtly inlaid with mother of pearl cherry blossom designs; Arabesque patterns are hand carved into the wood of armchairs; brightly hued stools are inspired by the shape of the oriental drum. For those who prefer sleeker designs, Debs' Contemporary collection is pure minimalism – the Pebble, a series of steel oval coffee tables in different sizes and tones, have become cult classics. Debs continues to travel to design fairs, where she mentors the new generation of Arab designers, helping them develop and promote their work.
Debs has showrooms in Saifi Village and a boutique in Zaitunay Bay.
Moukhalisieh Street, Saifi Village. Tel. 01-999 002, nadadebs.com

-55-

A GUIDE TO THE MIDDLE EAST'S MOST SOPHISTICATED CITY

Joe Kesrouani

A&D

THE TASTEMAKERS

YOUSSEF TOHME
THE THEORIST

HOW DOES BEIRUT INSPIRE YOU?

{ BEIRUT IS A CITY IN MOVEMENT, IN A STABLE IMBALANCE. IDEALS HAVE FALLEN AND FOR THE FIRST TIME, THERE IS SPACE FOR A NEW START. }

BOHO BEIRUT

A GUIDE TO THE MIDDLE EAST'S MOST SOPHISTICATED CITY

A & D

THE TASTEMAKERS:

YOUSSEF TOHME
The theorist

A rchitect Youssef Tohme, who studied architecture in Paris and worked with Jean Nouvel for several years, thinks about Lebanon in metaphorical images. "I think about the themes that represent the country's identity," he says. "The horizon, the envelope, the in-between. These themes take on another meaning in Lebanon. My architecture is at once violent and soft."

Tohme recently returned to Lebanon, after working on Nouvel's Louvre Abu Dhabi museum, seeking fresh inspiration. He builds pure, minimalist villas in the Lebanese mountains, embracing the landscape and sky. He also built the Université Saint-Joseph's Campus de l'Innovation et du Sport with 109 architectes: a white sculptural concrete mass perforated with slits of different sizes, evoking a modernist war citadel. Different building blocks are connected by passageways; the void between the blocks is what Tohme calls the "in-between." Inside, large staircases are reminiscent of the industrial labyrinth in Orson Welles' version of Kafka's *Trial*, with raw concrete and white steel banisters. Tohme incorporates subtle Oriental references, as Nouvel did at the Institut du Monde Arabe: One building is patterned with mosaic-style openings. "We are at the dawn of a new cultural identity," explains Tohme. "The flaws, the unstable balance interest me. Everyone is looking for one identity, but it doesn't exist."

BEST LEBANESE FOOD?
Boubouffe's shawarma sandwiches are incredible. Sayah is an amazing fish restaurant near the airport area. I order the raw fish with lemon and olive oil and the *meshoui fahem* (charcoal roasted fish).

YOUR FAVORITE CULTURAL SPACE?
Ashkal Alwan, my sister Christine's art foundation, for which I created the interior. It's like the Medici villa.

WATERING HOLE?
Dictateur is a true architect's bar. It reminds me of the atmosphere of the Beaux Arts in Paris.

BOHO BEIRUT

A GUIDE TO THE MIDDLE EAST'S MOST SOPHISTICATED CITY

BOUBOUFFE
MAR MITR STREET, ASHRAFIEH
TEL. 01-200 408 / 03-334 048
SAYAH
KHALDE, OLD SAIDA ROAD
TEL. 05-801 022 / 03-206 030
ASHKAL ALWAN
90 STREET, BUILDING 110,
JISR EL WATI
TEL. 01-423 879
DICTATEUR
BADAWI STREET, MAR MIKHAEL
TEL. 70-451 512

~~ADDRESS~~ BOOK YOUSSEF TOHME

A GUIDE TO THE MIDDLE EAST'S MOST SOPHISTICATED CITY

A&D

THE TASTEMAKERS

KAREN CHEKERDJIAN
THE NEO-TRADITIONALIST

HOW DOES BEIRUT INSPIRE YOU?

{ ITS CHAOS IS INSPIRING – THE DIRTY, THE BEAUTIFUL, THE UGLY, THE STRONG EMOTIONS THAT ARE ALWAYS FLOATING AROUND YOU. }

-63-

DON'T
OW HOW
TO

GUIDE TO THE MIDDLE EAST'S MOST SOPHISTICATED CITY

THE TASTEMAKERS:

KAREN CHEKERDJIAN
The neo-traditionalist

My approach is conceptual, experimental, and adapted to the local landscape," says designer Karen Chekerdjian. She studied at Milan's prestigious Domus Academy under the mentorship of Massimo Morozzi and is now a leader in the creation of a new design aesthetic in Lebanon. Mixing minimalist, cerebral designs with local patterns and materials and working with the country's artisans, she creates handmade copper chandeliers with mosaic patterns, wood, blown glass and brass. "What interests me is the history of an object," she says. Chekerdjian continues to travel, showing her work at industry fairs, but now she is based full-time in Beirut, where she has two children.

Chekerdjian's South Port boutique, a former metal warehouse, feels like a charming industrial atelier, with design objects scattered all around, brick walls and a shelf filled with the fine jams, cookies and pastas she loved the most while living in Italy. The motto of the store is written in large type: "Things we make, things we like."

WHY DID YOU OPEN IN SOPO?
I love this neighborhood. I chose it because it inspires me: It's the real Beirut. It's at once working-class and cutting-edge. There's a *manakish* (baked dough topped with thyme or cheese) place and the port restaurant where sailors and prostitutes hang out. My office is right above that street. And there's Lux café, which is perfect for having a drink and think.

BEST RESTAURANTS?
Yesterday I discovered Onno, an Armenian restaurant in Bourj Hammoud. It's delicious. They serve offal, sheep's brain, tongue, su beureg (cheese pie), and delicious dough dumplings in spicy yogurt.

WHERE DO YOU PICK YOUR GIFTS?
I like to pick up books at Papercup and objects at Orient 499. When I want to treat myself, I buy Comme des Garçons clothes at IF.

BOHO BEIRUT

A GUIDE TO THE MIDDLE EAST'S MOST SOPHISTICATED CITY

LUX
BOULOS FAYAD BUILDING, AL-GAMARIK STREET, PORT OF BEIRUT
TEL. 01-444 311
ONNO
AGHABIOS STREET, BOURJ HAMMOUD
TEL. 03-801 476
PAPERCUP
AGOPIAN BUILDING, PHARAON STREET, MAR MIKHAEL
TEL. 01-443 083
ORIENT 499
499 OMAR DAOUK STREET, HAMMOUD BUILDING, MINA EL-HOSN
TEL. 01-369 499
IF
ABDALLAH BEYHUM STREET, DOWNTOWN
TEL. 01-970 177

~~ADDRESS~~ BOOK

KAREN CHEKERDJIAN

A GUIDE TO THE MIDDLE EAST'S MOST SOPHISTICATED CITY

E

EAT

The great civilizations of the Levant have always celebrated the art of epicurean living. In Lebanon, the biblical land of milk and honey, fruits and vegetables grow abundantly on mountain groves and along the sea, mutton is deliciously fatty and robust, and fresh seafood is sold daily along the shore. Dense olive oil, aromatic mint, juicy tomatoes, crunchy cucumbers, tangy yogurt, figs like honey: The country's foods require little seasoning and are best enjoyed in their glorious freshness. The cuisine celebrates the land's rich flavors with light, subtle dishes that come in infinite variations depending on the season and region. All over the country, families gather weekly around gargantuan meals that last several hours and include mezzes, whole fish, grilled meats and lavish platters of fruit and sweets. Aromatic *arguiles* (water pipes) and *arak* (a strong, anise-flavored liquor), of course, are the necessary accompaniments. Mothers pass on closely guarded family secret recipes: delicious *kebbes* (ground lamb meat cooked with pine nuts), *yakhnes* (stews), complex salads and *warak enab* (stuffed vine leaves). The French Mandate also left traces in the local cuisine, and there are many delicious French restaurants in Beirut. But while many traditions have been lost with modernity and the globalization of fast food, several food entrepreneurs are fighting to sustain local farmers and keep traditional recipes alive. A fine wine industry is also blooming – the Musar and Massaya brands are particularly worth sampling. And while today's generation is more calorie-conscious than our ancestors were, people still like to meet for long meals. Beirut's vibrant restaurant scene reflects this passion for all things culinary.

A GUIDE TO THE MIDDLE EAST'S MOST SOPHISTICATED CITY

EAT

01 *Abdel Wahab

It is not easy to find true Lebanese cuisine outside of private homes but Abdel Wahab, a traditional restaurant near the Albergo Hotel, serves all the classics. *Kibbeh nayeh* (raw lamb's meat), *sawda nayyeh* (raw sheep's liver) and *samkeh harra* (spicy fish) are necessary treats.

Tip: On a balmy night ask for a table on the rooftop terrace.
- Address: Abdel Wahab El Inglizi Street, Achrafieh
- Tel. 01-200 550

02 *Casablanca

If you ask any artist, designer, architect or gallerist what their favorite restaurant is, they invariably mention Casablanca. This traditional Levantine villa overlooking the Corniche is decorated with fun, pop art–style touches. The restaurant serves light, fresh Asian-inspired dishes: fresh seafood tartare, botarga pasta and flavorful salads. Enjoy the view of the Mediterranean from the tables near the arcade windows.

Tip: Casablanca serves a very popular weekend brunch with scrambled eggs, bagels and a particularly appreciated mimosa.
- Address: Dar el Mreisseh Street
- Tel. 01-369 334 / 03-856 111

03 *Chez Sophie

After living in Europe and Canada, Sophie Tabet recently moved back to Lebanon with her Italian husband Marco Marangi and opened this elegant restaurant in an old Lebanese house. With its high ceilings, arcades and brick walls, it's the perfect backdrop for Tabet's gastronomical cuisine. Inspired by the changing seasons, she creates complex dishes contrasting flavors, textures and colors, such as a paella-inspired risotto and a duck and foie gras dish. And, after studying the art of risotto making in Italy for one year, she is a true pro.

Tip: Ask Tabet's husband for Italian wine recommendations. He is an expert sommelier.
- Address: Main Street, Mar Mikheal
- Tel. 01-566 991
- W.chezsophie-lb.com

04 *Couqley

For a typical French brasserie dinner, Couqley serves *moules marinières*, hand-cut fries, duck salad, *escargots* and *croque monsieur*. In this former artisan's workshop, the mosaic tiled floor and zinc bar create a casual, nostalgic ambiance. If you're on a date, ask for the *côte de boeuf pour deux*, served with deliciously buttery potatoes and creamy sauce *Béarnaise*; follow with *crème brûlée* or *mousse au chocolat*.

Tip: Couqley serves brunch too, so head there on weekends after a leisurely stroll in Gemmayze.
- Address: The Alleyway, Gouraud Street, Gemmayze
- Tel. 01-442 678

05 *Frosty Palace*

Zalfa Naufal is notorious for her rich, flavorful cakes, which she sells at her sister's Papercup bookstore. Naufal has finally opened her own restaurant: Frosty Palace, a sophisticated diner in Mar Mikhael that serves classics such as burgers, pancakes, salads and sandwiches alongside homemade ice creams and cakes. Naufal, who studied cooking at the Cordon Bleu school in Sydney and gelato making in Italy, is a true gourmet and emphasizes fresh, natural ingredients. And the faded diner décor, with its booths, frosty blue tones and retro tunes, is ideal for a Grease-style night out.

Tip: Before dinner, pick up a few magazines from Papercup right across the street.
- Address: Pharaon Street, Mar Mikhael
- Tel. 01-449 595

06 *Ginette*

Ginette is the place of choice for ladies who lunch in skinny leggings, perfect blowouts and Pierre Hardy heels. This concept store, designed by Raed Abillama's firm, offers handpicked clothes and accessories from around the world, including the sought after (and steeply priced) USM Swiss watches and the Australian botanics beauty brand AESOP. The café serves *tartines* made with the very honorable Poilâne bread – flown in from Paris- as well as health-conscious options for those watching their calories, such as quinoa and arugula salads. But the rest of us will follow with desserts from one of the best pastry chefs in Beirut, Nayla Audi of Oslo. Her rich flourless chocolate cake was featured in Pierre Hermé's book on chocolate, and it's pure decadence.

Tip: The second floor space, curated by the Japanese gallery Nanzuka Underground, shows rotating art exhibitions.
- Address: Gouraud Street, Gemmayze
- Tel. 01-570 440
- W.ginette-beirut.com

BOHO BEIRUT

07 *Gossip Café

Shopping and salads are a classic for ladies who lunch; and at this aptly named new restaurant, they are combined with a scrumptious menu. After picking slim jeans, bikinis or stilettos at Aïzone, kick back at the sleek Gossip Café. Order a club sandwich or a Caesar salad and a diet Coke. For those in need of higher forms of enlightenment, there are art books by Taschen and Assouline and specialty magazines.

Tip: Skip lunch altogether and sample the tasty desserts: chocolate éclair, profiteroles, banana split, perhaps?
- Address: ABC Mall, Dbayeh
- Tel. 04-417 217
- W.aishti.com

08 *Lux

In the hot new SoPo district, this modern brasserie designed by Karim Bekdache offers fresh, delicious dishes and finely crafted cocktails. Order a mix of plates and share. The lightly fried seafood, whole cooked fish and fragrant pastas are musts. The salads come from owner Johnny Farah's mountain grove and are lightly dressed with lemon and the finest olive oil; the cocktails are made with fresh herbs such as rosemary, basil and lemongrass.

Tip: Ask for the rashad salad, a delicate and peppery green you will not find anywhere else.
- Address: Al Gamarik Street, Port of Beirut
- Tel. 01-566 991

EAT

09 *Momo

Suspended over the Majidiye mosque in the jewelry souks, Momo is a cool spot for dining and people watching over drinks. Opened by Mourad Mazouz, the Paris and London nightlife and dining guru who also owns Sketch and Andy Wahloo, this is the ultimate restaurant-cum-nightclub. You'll get Moroccan classics such as couscous and tajines, served in a fantastical neo-oriental décor created by designer and architect Annabel Kassar. After dinner the lights are dimmed and scantily clad types flood in to dance to the beats of the best DJs in town.

Tip: Make sure you ask for a table on the suspended garden.
- Address: Jewelry n 7 Street, Beirut Souks
- Tel. 01-999 767

10 *Osteria

When you need a laid-back spot to have a glass of wine and a nice homemade meal, there is Osteria. At this small Mar Mikhael restaurant, an Italian lady cooks rustic Italian recipes while her Lebanese husband plays rocking sounds. The generous wine list will keep you going through the night, when the eatery turns into a lively bar. The rustic platters of Italian charcuteries and cheeses are the perfect accompaniments to an aperitif.

Tip: Ask for the vegetarian *tourtes*, the house specialty.
- Address: Nahr Street, Mar Mikhael
- Tel. 01-566 175

11 *Papercup

For all of us who need a morning, afternoon and early evening pick-me-up, there is Papercup. This charming Mar Mikhael bookstore offers niche magazines and beautiful art books, which you can read on the spot in the tiny café area. Order excellent tea from local brand Awan and the freshly-made chocolate chip or banana cakes baked by Zalfa Naufal, the sister of Papercup's owner Rania. The traditional mosaic tiles were foraged from the Blatt Chaya factory, and the wooden book-cover chandelier is the boutique's trademark logo.

Tip: Watch out for book signing events or artist events – the party often spills out onto the sidewalk.
- Address: Pharaon Street, Mar Mikheal
- Tel. 01-443 083
- W.papercupstore.com

12 *Sweet Tea

It has become tricky to find authentic French pastries anywhere in the world – including in France itself. At Sweet Tea, the local pastry outpost of Le Meurice's chef Yannick Allèno in the Beirut Souks, those with a sweet tooth will be delighted. The signature *pain au chocolat* is filled – and covered – with thick, crunchy, dark chocolate; the Mont-Blanc is perfumed with delicate chestnuts and an airy whipped cream; and the lemon tart is light and flavorful.

Tip: If you have an important lunch, book a table at the nearby S.T.A.Y, three-Michelin-starred Allèno's fine gastronomic restaurant.
- Address: Fakhry Bey Street, Beirut Souks
- Tel. 01-999 757

EAT

13 * The Gathering

When a team of restaurateurs found three old Lebanese houses, including a structure dating from the 16th century. and an antique well in a cobblestoned courtyard, they decided to restore and highlight the structures. With The Gathering restaurants, they have created an oasis in the middle of Saifi's masses of concrete and stone. Following a 100 percent ecological ethos, the team has created a wine bar, a butcher grill and an Italian trattoria. And as the Slow Food guidelines advise, the restaurants mostly serve ingredients from local farms, but there are also imported delicacies – prosciutto, fine cheeses and an international wine list. The atmosphere is particularly festive on the outdoor terrace connecting the three restaurants.

Tip: The Gathering doesn't take reservations, so try to get there early to get a table.
- Address: Pasteur Street, Gemmayze
- Tel. 01-566 196

14 * Tawlet

When Kamal Mouzawak brought together Lebanese farmers at the Souk el Tayeb market, he started a small Slow Food revolution in a country that had started to lose its ancestral traditions. At Tawlet, his quaint Mar Mikhael eatery, he hires women from different regions of the country to concoct traditional dishes. Every day, a different area is represented, illustrating the complex nuances of a land rich in local traditions and geographies. The buffet is composed of salads, *mezzes* (small appetizers) and stews, and of course dessert. *Knefeh*, a melting sweet cheese with a crunchy crust saturated in sugar syrup, is especially regal. Those who want to learn new recipes can sign up for the weekly cooking classes with the master.

Tip: Ask for the homemade lemonade – with a dash of rose water. It's refreshing and delicious.
- Address: Nahr Street, Mar Mikhael
- Tel. 01-448 129
- W.tawlet.com

BEST OF STREETFOOD

As the city is colonized by fast-food chains, the authentic street food vendors of yesteryear are vanishing. Anissa Helou, Middle Eastern cuisine specialist cookbook author, journalist and chef, tells us where to get a taste of the real Beirut.

*Matem Al-Soussi

Lebanese breakfasts are savory affairs on the whole. Fatteh, a multi-layered dish made up of toasted pita, boiled chickpeas, yoghurt and toasted pine nuts, is my favorite. And there is no one who makes a better fatteh than Al Soussi who, like Hajj Tabbara, has been boiling chickpeas in huge pots and serving fatteh, as well as hummus and fool, for years to faithful customers.
- Address: Dr. Shahadeh Street, Mar Elias, Zeydaniyeh.
- Tel. 03-927 421 (open 6am to 2pm)

*Hanna

There may be better-known names for ice cream, but Hanna is simply the best. Old Hanna Mitri has been serving freshly made ice cream in the same little shop in Ashrafieh for nearly 60 years, with his faithful wife by his side. The choice is limited to a few flavors: rose water, pistachio, almond, milk, lemon and seasonal fruit. Every single one is sensational.
- Address: Mar Mitr Street, Ashrafieh
- Tel. 01-322 723

*Falafel Tabbara

Falafel has gone global now and you find good falafel in London, New York and Paris, but none is as exciting as the falafel made in this small, modest stall in a side street down from the Bristol Hotel. The owner, Al-Haj Mohammed Tabbara, mans the till, while his falafel maker, who's been with him for very many years, makes the best sandwich ever, filled with falafel prepared à l'Egyptienne, i.e., with broad beans only, and generous amounts of fresh herbs and pickles.
- Address: Lyon Street, Hamra
- Tel. 01-350 821

EAT

BOHO BEIRUT

KARIM HAIDAR
THE POETRY OF FLAVORS

Self-taught chef Karim Haidar fell in love with cooking as a child as his grandmother prepared inventive dishes in the family kitchen. He went on to study, practice and teach law in Paris, but he returned to his initial passion and opened 'Au 29' in 1999, reinventing Lebanese classics. A few years later, Haidar became the chef at Fakhreddine, London's oldest Lebanese restaurant, where he continued to develop contemporary creations such as orange blossom hommos and lobster frikeh. He also created the menu for Liza in Paris, launched a bakery and catering service, wrote several cookery books and even children's stories. Today Haidar owns three restaurants in Paris, works as a consultant worldwide, and converts traditionalists to his poetic vision at Zabad, his first Beirut restaurant. Zabad, which means 'foam of the sea,' is the ultimate realization of Haidar's dream: to celebrate Lebanon's rich traditions and products, and to infuse them with fresh, daring creativity. Karim's vision of the terroir is deeply philosophical. "It's the link between the soil and geography on one hand, and human sweat on the other," he says. His dishes unfold like so many narratives of the Lebanon's history, landscapes and people. He serves the country's crisp, flavorful zucchini naked but for a hint of lemon juice and salt. "This is my message," he says. "We have magnificent zucchini. Why spend hours degrading it when we can savor its full taste?" The chef also uses the bottarga traditionally served on garlic toast in myriad unexpected combinations. Its salty, pungent flavor mingles with tart green plums, sweet strawberries or wild thyme in Zabad's playful salads. Throughout these culinary explorations, Haidar has rediscovered the country he had left in 1985. "I love the insanity, the exuberance," he says. Beirut has given me the taste for life more than any other city I have lived in."

THE TASTEMAKERS

SOPHIE TABET
THE GOURMANDE

HOW DOES BEIRUT INSPIRE YOU?

{ I REALLY LOVED FINALLY FEELING AT HOME AFTER EXTENSIVE TRAVELS! I HAD ALWAYS WANTED TO OPEN MY FIRST RESTAURANT IN LEBANON. I WANT TO CHANGE THINGS HERE. }

-81-

chez sophie

THE TASTEMAKERS:

SOPHIE TABET
The Gourmande

"The secret of cooking really is love," says Sophie Tabet, the young chef and co-owner of Chez Sophie. At the Paul Bocuse Institute she also learned the importance of hard work and professionalism. Tabet rapidly went on to train at L'Astrance in Paris and Nadia Santini's in Italy. Missing her homeland, she moved back to Lebanon where she opened Chez Sophie with her brother Samir, a hotel management graduate, and her husband, Italian sommelier Marco Marangi. The restaurant, located on the ground floor of a Lebanese house, is elegant and classic, with arcades and a neutral palette of colors. There, Tabet mixes French and Italian traditions and finds inspiration in seasonal products to create complex, rich flavors and colors. The pasta is freshly crafted on order; the risotto comes in surprising flavors such as lapsang souchong, lemon or smoked mozzarella. Tabet also supports local food artisans and enjoys shopping for fresh Lebanese produce at Souk el Tayeb, the local farmers' market.

BEST RESTAURANT?

La Table d'Alfred is impeccable; the chef really emphasizes the products he uses and his dishes are flavorful. At Souk el Tayeb I buy edible flowers, wild thyme, fig jam and – the best! – *zaatar manakish*.

A RECOMMENDATION FOR WINE SHOPPING?

Our friend Louis Tannous imports fine wines from Burgundy, for private orders.

BEST DESSERTS?

Sweet Tea is a lovely café, with a private garden-terrace. I like their lemon tart and Saint-Honoré.

BEST LEBANESE FOOD?

Fadel in Bikfaya. The mezzes are tasty, and you sit in the mountains, breathing fresh air.

LA TABLE D'ALFRED
SURSOCK STREET, ASHRAFIEH
TEL. 01-203 036
SOUK EL TAYEB
TRABLOS STREET, BEIRUT SOUKS
TEL. 01-442 664
FADEL
NAAS VILLAGE, NAAS
TEL. 04-980 979
SWEET TEA
FAKHRY BEY STREET, BEIRUT SOUKS
TEL. 01-999 757

ADDRESS BOOK
SOPHIE TABET

A GUIDE TO THE MIDDLE EAST'S MOST SOPHISTICATED CITY

EAT

THE TASTEMAKERS

HUSSEIN HADID

THE INNOVATOR

HOW DOES BEIRUT INSPIRE YOU?

{ ALTHOUGH I HAVE TRAVELED ALL MY LIFE, I ALWAYS HAD A DEEP LOVE FOR BEIRUT — THE OLD MARKETS, THE SUNSHINE, THE NICE PEOPLE, THE BEAUTIFUL LANDSCAPES... }

BOHO BEIRUT

-87-

A GUIDE TO THE MIDDLE EAST'S MOST SOPHISTICATED CITY

THE TASTEMAKERS:

HUSSEIN HADID
The innovator

Hussein Hadid roams markets in Iran, Iraq, Gulf countries, Syria and Lebanon looking for fragrant herbs, dried fruits and hot spices for his inventive dishes. He rubs a leg of lamb with pomegranate skin powder and molasses, adds herbs and spices to falafels, or incorporates sour cherries into a pilaf or pasta dish. Hadid is Lebanon's most prestigious caterer, a fixture at weddings and cocktail parties known for his exquisite, sophisticated food. At his industrial home kitchen, he also whips up feasts for groups of guests – from 10 to 30 – including flowers, wines and fine desserts such as *halawet el jebn* with apricots or white chocolate pudding – a cult favorite. A childhood in the UK, studies at the French Culinary Institute New York and experiences throughout the world have shaped a truly global vision – but Hadid still builds his menus on the French or Italian classics "with a twist." For those in need of a New York style juicy burger, he has opened the upscale BRGR Co., where he serves perfect prime Australian patties topped with aged cheddar and oh-so-decadent shakes.

FOOD SHOPPING?
At Aziz I buy cheeses, oil, balsamic vinegar, truffles, caviar and *foie gras*.
FAVORITE BEACH?
Bamboo Bay, a small unpretentious beach in the South where you can tan in peace.
A SPOT TO PICK UP GIFTS?
Orient 499, where there is an infinite choice of refined Oriental inspired objects for the home, clothes, jewels and beauty products.

BOHO BEIRUT

AZIZ
GROUND FLOOR, ABI AAD BUILDING, FAKHREDDINE STREET, MINA EL-HOSN
TEL. 01-358 000
W.AZIZSARL.COM

BAMBOO BAY
SAIDA HIGHWAY, JIYEH
TEL. 03-513 888
W.BAMBOO-BAY.COM

ORIENT 499
HAMMOUD BUILDING, 499 OMAR DAOUK STREET, MINA EL-HOSN
TEL. 01-369 499

~~ADDRESS~~ BOOK

HUSSEIN HADID

A GUIDE TO THE MIDDLE EAST'S MOST SOPHISTICATED CITY

EAT

D

DRINK

Beirut has always been a legendary center of fun, and locals go to great lengths to maintain this glittery reputation. For cheap prestige, some regulars at posh bars rent champagne magnums for the night, sometimes even asking for the accompanying fireworks. Women dance on bar counters, couches, speakers and tables, flaunting their mini-dresses – and what's underneath, shaking their artfully straightened manes for extra impact. Men, their hair plastered with shiny gels, their muscles highlighted by tailored blazers, roam the rooms seeking prey and sending doo-doo shots (a local invention, basically a dirty martini with Tabasco in a shot glass) to the prettiest girls. It can sometimes seem challenging to find good music and a laid-back crowd in this circus-like scene, but you just need to push further. Beirut has a gritty nightlife scene, brilliant indie bands and wild dance parties. You'll find minuscule holes in the wall where people chatter spontaneously, semi-legal underground party spots, beach raves and delicious, fresh cocktails. Until recently smoking was allowed and bars were filled with thick clouds of nicotine; even with the new ban smokers continue to puff away, perpetuating the Lebanese tradition of ignoring laws and regulation. For a typical Lebanese night, start with a nap; follow with late dinner, and don't plan to hit the bar before 11p.m. Also, pace yourself. You'll be going out every single day.

DRINK

01 *Angry Monkey

For those nostalgic of college drinking nights there is Angry Monkey, where Australians and Americans meet up to discuss the strange vagaries of Beirut – inefficient driving codes, traffic, corrupt policemen. There's a wide selection of beers; burgers, soft-shell crab and steak satisfy late-night appetites. The marshmallow roasting at the lit-up copper bar should initiate interesting drunk chatter.

Tip: Want to watch the football match? This is the place to be.
- Address: Gouraud Street, Gemmayze
- Tel. 01-566 376

02 *Bardo

Beirut is an unofficial gay capital – homosexuality is still illegal but several bars and clubs offer havens for singles or groups. Bardo, a sleek Hamra bar with chill electronic music, is the city's best-known gay-friendly spot and is also a great place to get a good drink and bite (from chicken souvlaki to teryaki) and make new friends.

Tip: Bardo turns into a small club as the night progresses, so plan for a big evening out.
- Address: Mexico Street, Clemenceau
- Tel. 01-340 060

03 *Behind the Green Door

This lounge was named after a seventies porn film, and, behind the heavy green doors, the vibe is appropriately debaucherous. Couples flirt on the velvet couches, excited young people swing on the dancing pole, groups dance closely on the tiny dance floor. DJs play everything from Brigitte Bardot to Sonic Youth – the sexier the better. The light is dimmed; here the motto is, unsurprisingly, "What happens behind the green door stays behind the green door."

Tip: This is where many Beirut nights end. Don't worry if it's 2 a.m. on a Wednesday. There's a party at Behind.
- Address: Main Street, Mar Mikhael
- Tel. 01-565 656

04 *B018

B018 is Beirut's most legendary nightclub. The pioneer project of architect Bernard Khoury, it is a dark and underground cell built beneath a flat parking space. Inside, the moody atmosphere, tomb-shaped benches and convertible roof create a dramatic setting. Here the dancing is hard and parties never end before dusk.

Tip: In Beirut, do as the Beirutis do: Follow the boozing with a stop at *manakish* chain Zaatar w Zeit, where you will cross fellow party mates munching on cheese or thyme breads and planning the day's beach program.
- Address: Karantina, Beirut
- Tel. 01-580 018

A GUIDE TO THE MIDDLE EAST'S MOST SOPHISTICATED CITY

DRINK

Coop d'Etat

05 *Centrale

At the end of a long narrow alley of gardenia bushes, a steel structure encases a traditional stone house: Centrale, designed by architect Bernard Khoury. On the ground floor, a restaurant hosts small and large parties for delicious and light fare – in the summer, dinner is also served in the jasmine-filled garden. The elevator–a sort of vertical tomb–takes you to the bar, a tunnel-like room where the retractable roof opens up on balmy days. While you sip a scrumptious concoction and nibble on an appetizer (seared scallops? Tuna tartare? Artichoke salad?), breathe the Beirut summer air and look up at the stars.

Tip: This place gets packed quickly, so head there early and leave before the crowd takes over.
- Address: Mar Maroun Street, Saifi/Ashrafieh
- Tel. 01-575 858

06 *Coop d'Etat

Coop d'Etat is a rooftop bar in lower Gemmayze owned by an American journalist and his friends. There, locals and expats grab a caipirova, a hot dog sandwich and cigarettes and kick back with their pals overlooking the Mediterranean.

Tip: The restaurant downstairs – Em Nazih – serves delicious Lebanese food – *manakish*, salads, grilled meats and even a plat du jour.
- Address: Pasteur Street, Gemmayze
- Tel. 01-564 118

BOHO BEIRUT

07 *Demo

When in the mood to discuss Existentialism, the Nouvelle Vague and the Arab Spring, Demo is a trusted refuge. Owned by journalist and playwright Tarek Mourad and his musician friend Nabil Saliba of Slutterhouse, this is where the city's creatives and intellectuals meet for a solid cocktail, good music, toasted sandwiches and perhaps a little drunk dancing. Ask about concerts and special events. And order the oh-so-fresh ginger gin gimlet.

Tip: If you're driving, you won't find any parking around the bar. Just give the car to one of the valets on the main Gemmayze strip.
- Address: **Rue du Liban, Gemmayze**
- Tel. 03-958 504

08 *Dictateur

When a group of young architects built the Dictateur bar in a narrow Mar Mikhael street, the *tout-creative* Beirut was swiftly converted. The industrial, bunker-like structure is divided into several sections – a garden, a bar, a terrace and a lounge, so dancing from room to room is absolutely acceptable – after a few caipirinas at the bar, that is. The style is scavenged-chic, with furniture found at the flea market, a toilet bowl-turned-flower pot and recycled metal and wood fixtures.

Tip: Dictateur serves sandwiches and salads, too- the weekend brunch parties were quite wild, with barbecue meats, freshly made thyme and cheese *manakish* - and of course cocktails.
- Address: **Badawi Street, Mar Mikhael**
- Tel. 03-251 512

DRINK

EM Chill

09 *DRM

The Democratic Republic of Music is a great addition to Beirut's music scene. This large, gritty underground venue hosts concerts almost daily, from jazz to blues, rock and traditional Arabic music. There are even salsa lessons followed by dance parties for those who want to really shake it. The sound is great, there's valet parking, and you can order pre-concert snacks.

Tip: This isn't a cocktail kind of place, so stick to basics like beer, wine and vodka-tonics.
- Address: Sourati Street, Hamra
- Tel. 01-752 202

10 *EM Chill

When in need of a fresh beer at the end of a workday, head to EM Chill, a spot in Mar Mikhael that, as its name indicates, is super relaxed – with reggae, jazz and friendly staff. Creative types set up their laptops at the bar and chat while munching on finger food; the club downstairs hosts concerts and events and free film projections on Mondays.

Tip: For those who need a Wi-Fi spot during the day, there's breakfast and lunch, too.
- Address: Main Street, Mar Mikhael
- Tel. 01-565 313

BOHO BEIRUT

11 *Torino Express*

One of the first – and coolest – bars to open in Gemmayze, this former picture-framing workshop is still a daily meeting spot for artsy types. Andreas Boulos, the handsome German-Lebanese owner, stands at the turntables playing a heady mix of post-punk, Arabic classics, sixties rock and funk. The fresh cocktails are addictive. This is a great place to start the night with a mojito, carrots and nuts – do head there early before the crowds take over.

Tip: If you're peckish, order a melting panino with an Almaza beer – the perfect snack before a big night out.
- Address: Gouraud Street, Gemmayze
- Tel. 03-611 101

UNDERGROUND PARTIES

If you want to party with the locals, there is always something going on in Beirut – house parties, beach parties, rooftop parties, pop-up parties… These are two of the city's best underground bashes:
The Beirut Groove Collective was launched in 2009 by two DJs and their friends who organized events inspired by the underground funk and soul parties of the seventies and Don Cornelius' iconic Soul Train dance show. The Collective is now active worldwide, promoting African-inspired music from far-flung places, spinning in Paris or Dubai and inviting legends like Nikodemus to the Middle East. When the BGC is on, there are MCs, DJs, hip-hop acts, colorful crowds- and most importantly, a great warm vibe. If techno is your cup of tea the Cotton Candy parties happen in secret and attract the wildest crowds in town to empty apartments, basements or rooftops – through word-of-mouth only. There, turntable masters Djette and the Underdolls, among others, keep the party moving for endless nights.

DRINK

THE TASTEMAKERS

CHARLES KETTANEH
THE THINKER

HOW DOES BEIRUT INSPIRE YOU?

{ BEIRUT NEVER KEEPS YOU INDIFFERENT. IT ALWAYS PROVOKES YOU. IT'S NOT NECESSARILY POSITIVE, NOR HEALTHY. FOR SOME REASON, WHATEVER BEIRUT DOES TO YOU FEELS ILLEGAL, ABNORMAL, AND THIS PROVOKES A REACTION. SOMETIMES THIS REACTION CAN BECOME AN INSPIRATION. }

-101-

DRINK

THE TASTEMAKERS:
CHARLES KETTANEH
The Thinker

Architect Charles Kettaneh has lived in Paris and New York; after the recession paralyzed the job market he moved back to Beirut seeking new opportunities. He started working at a local firm and dreamed of opening a beer garden in the city; he missed Brooklyn's boho atmosphere. When his brother-in-law purchased an old commercial space in Mar Mikhael, Kettaneh and three partners–two architects, Maram Attallah and Mardig Troshagerian, and a restaurateur, Hady Salhab–decided to convert the structure into a bar. Located in a hidden narrow backstreet, the building originally served as a garage and store. The partners divided it into different areas (a bar, a lounge, a garden and a mezzanine), creating an open courtyard in the center. They filled it with wooden antique chairs scavenged at the Basta flea market, created a chandelier with mechanics' lamps and huge trapezoid wooden structures that cast a soft light above the bar. The team also recycled the steel floors into plant containers where lemon, kumquat and herb trees are now scattered throughout-the fruits are used to concoct delicious cocktails. Now that Charlie, as his friends call him, has his own watering hole, he no longer feels the need to go back to Brooklyn.

BEST HANGOUTS?
I really like Coop d'Etat and the restaurant in the building's basement, Em Nazih. Artists and expats hang out there; it's unpretentious and fun. The restaurant serves traditional Lebanese cooking that's hearty and simple. I also love Zico House, an old house turned into a cultural center that hosts book signings, art events and parties. At Angry Monkey, a Gemmayze bar that looks like a boat lounge, there are always American and Australian tourists and the cocktails are nice.

BEST GALLERY?
I love my friend Lea Sednaoui's The Running Horse.

DANCE SPOT?
B018 is the only decent nightclub in Beirut. Art Lounge has good concerts; I saw DJ Diplo and several Lebanese bands there.

COOP D'ETAT
SAIFI URBAN GARDENS, PASTEUR STREET, GEMMAYZEH
TEL. 71-134 173
EM NAZIH
PASTEUR STREET, GEMMAYZE
TEL.01-560 738
ZICO HOUSE
SPEARS STREET, SANAYEH
TEL. 01-746 769
W.ZICOHOUSE.ORG
ANGRY MONKEY
GOURAUD STREET, GEMMAYZE
TEL.01-566 376
THE RUNNING HORSE
SHUKRI AL-KHOURY STREET, KHODR SECTOR, KARANTINA
TEL.01-562 778
W.THERUNNINGHORSEART.COM
BO18
KARANTINA
TEL. 01-580 018
W.BO18.COM

ART LOUNGE
RIVER BRIDGE, KARANTINA
TEL. 03-997 676
W.ARTLOUNGE.NET

A GUIDE TO THE MIDDLE EAST'S MOST SOPHISTICATED CITY

~~ADDRESS~~ BOOK
CHARLES KETTANEH

DRINK

THE TASTEMAKERS

OLIVIER GASNIER DU- PARC *AND* YOUSEF HA- RATI- *THE DE- BAUCHEES*

HOW DOES BEIRUT INSPIRE YOU?

{ WE ARE THE ONES WHO INSPIRE BEIRUT! YOU NEED TO KNOW THAT. }

-107-

MAN CREATES HIS OWN GOD FOR HIMSELF

A GUIDE TO THE MIDDLE EAST'S MOST SOPHISTICATED CITY

LUCIFER

DRINK

THE TASTEMAKERS:

OLIVIER GASNIER DUPARC AND YOUSEF HARATI–
The Debauchees

Olivier Gasnier Duparc, from Paris, was managing an international flower distributing network in Beirut; Yousef Harati, from Beirut, was working at a major advertising firm. When the two met and bonded after the July 2006 War, people were coming back to the country and were hungry for parties. The inseparable duo started organizing small gatherings in Hotel Albergo's Jacques Garcia-designed lobby; some were costume parties, some were not - most were memorable in their wildness. Soon the bad boys opened their own lounge, Behind the Green Door, inspired by the eponymous seventies art porn film. The city's young and cool, and well-informed tourists, came to dance around the poles, drink champagne and smoke cigarettes and cigars on the red velvet banquettes. Today the bar is overcrowded with the type of people who never want the nights to end, including a slew of attractive girls in tight designer dresses. Once you've passed the bouncers and massive green doors you're that much closer to them – and that's what Olivier and Yousef love most about their job. And when they're not chatting up Swedish models, the boys are organizing massive dance parties at larger venues with the world's best DJs, including Diplo, The Magician and Yuksek.

FAVORITE RESTAURANT?
Burgundy is the best high-end restaurant in the city, and the wine list is spectacular.
A SPOT FOR ONE LAST DRINK?
The bar at the Four Seasons. It's very cozy, very quiet and you never see anyone you know – a rarity in this city. It's the perfect place to caress a pretty girl's thigh after a romantic evening.
SHOPPING?
The boys like to shop at Aïshti, where Olivier buys Martin Margiela turtlenecks and cardigans and Yousef gets Tod's loafers, Seven jeans and tops by Zadig & Voltaire.
BEST POOL IN TOWN?
Le Gray Hotel's infinity pool, which looks over Martyrs' Square, the city and the Mediterranean.

BOHO BEIRUT

A GUIDE TO THE MIDDLE EAST'S MOST SOPHISTICATED CITY

DRINK

BURGUNDY
752 GOURAUD STREET, SAIFI VILLAGE
TEL. 01-999 820
W.BURGUNDYBEIRUT.COM
FOUR SEASONS HOTEL
WAFIC SINNO AVE. MINA EL-HOSN
TEL. 01-761 000
WWW.FOURSEASONS.COM
AÏSHTI
MOUTRAN STREET, DOWNTOWN
TEL. 01-991 111
W.AISHTI.COM
LE GRAY HOTEL
WEYGAND STREET, DOWNTOWN
TEL. 01-971 111
W.CAMPBELLGRAYHOTELS.COM

BOHO BEIRUT

ADDRESS BOOK

OLIVIER GASNIER DUPARC
AND YOUSEF HARATI

A GUIDE TO THE MIDDLE EAST'S MOST SOPHISTICATED CITY

DRINK

S

SHOP

Many men claim that Lebanese women are the most beautiful in the world. Perhaps that is because appearance is such an important aspect of the local culture. During the long summer, women oil their bodies in coconut-scented ointments, swim long laps and read Vogue and Bazaar and munch on fresh watermelon by the sea. Post-beach, they wear fragrant gardenia or jasmine necklaces sold on the streets, their silky hair shining against their golden skin. Hairdressers and manicurists are an essential part of many women's weekly routine; diets, Botox and sometimes plastic surgery are local essentials. With the culture's important focus on social gatherings, dressing up is also taken very seriously. There are scarce chances you'll see women wearing the same dress to more than one party. Thankfully, the city's sartorial offerings are aplenty. Lebanon's designers, couturiers and jewelers take inspiration from Paris' couture heritage and the rich Oriental traditions to create feminine and sophisticated collections. Elie Saab and Rabih Kayrouz, internationally renowned couturiers who create breathtaking evening gowns, have both joined the Chambre Syndicale de la Couture in Paris and have dressed countless celebrities. Now the new generation is working in a range of styles, from eco-conscious to avant-garde and lavish, offering something for every woman.

A GUIDE TO THE MIDDLE EAST'S MOST SOPHISTICATED CITY

SHOP

01 *Aïshti

Cocktail parties, gallery openings, weddings, dance parties...The question "what to wear" is a daily source of angst for Beiruti women. Thankfully there is Aïshti, the luxury department store filled with marvels from Etro, Chanel, Missoni, Prada and contemporary brands such as Seven and Marc by Marc Jacobs. There you'll find "it" bags and shoes galore, fanciful accessories and hard-to-find beauty brands such as Bobbi Brown and L'Artisan Parfumeur. At People Café, the creamy hot chocolate, crunchy caramelized banana tart and sweeping views of the city's glitterati turn a dull afternoon into a feast.

Tip: For those in need of a beauty fix, the adjacent spa has soothing and beautifying treatments in a peaceful, elegant setting. Try the Dermalogica Environmental Control facial – especially after a maddening day in Beirut traffic.

- Address: El Moutrane Street, Downtown Beirut
- Tel. 01-991 111
- W.aishti.com

02 *Artisanat du Liban et d'Orient

The designer Nadia Khoury Kemp, who pioneered the Lebanese artisanal movement, reinvents traditional Oriental costume with luxurious materials and vibrant colors–adding a contemporary touch. There are silk dresses in jewel tones, serwals in different cuts and colors and unique shirts in antique silk that are luxurious classics. This is also a great place to pick up a gift, such as silk bathrobes and slippers, children's clothes, books about Oriental culture, soaps, candles and perfumes. Dab a drop of amber essence on your wrists and neck before a summer night out; its scent is heady and sensual.

Tip: Before you leave the shop, make sure you go out on the raw concrete terrace to admire the Mediterranean horizon.

- Address: Corniche, Ain el Mreisseh
- Tel. 01-362 610
- W.artisansduliban.com

BOHO BEIRUT

03 *Elie Saab

Lebanon's most famous couturier is known for dressing stars like Halle Berry and Scarlett Johansson in luxurious and modern goddess dresses. But if you have yet to find an occasion for your wedding gown, the designer sells his ready-to-wear collection, a smart, toned-down version of his couture at his downtown boutique. Blazers come in rich hues, sweaters are embroidered with sequins, dresses reveal a shoulder line or a deep décolletage. In no time Elie Saab transforms women into Oriental seductresses- for an office meeting or a night at Le Baron.

Tip: Pick up a bottle of the ultra-feminine perfume, Le Parfum. This seductive flowery and woodsy elixir is the creation of prestige parfumeur Francis Kurkdjian. With its orange blossom, jasmine and honey notes, it is reminiscent of a luscious spring evening in Beirut.
- Address: Bab Idriss Street, Downtown
- Tel. 01-981 982
- W.eliesaab.com

04 *If

When you see artsy types clad in head-to-toe black, chances are they are IF fanatics. Since the eighties, the store has been introducing conceptual brands such as Martin Margiela, Comme des Garçons, Ann Demeulemeester and Rick Owens to the Lebanese. It also carries Johnny Farah leatherware, Rosie Abourous rings, and the urban-chic collections of Danish designer Ivan Grundahl, whose tailored white shirts and razor-sharp black skirts make for perfect office staples. And if you're hooked, IF now has four outposts in Beirut, one in Dubai and one in New York.

Tip: Head to the store's new boutique in the SoPo area, which is flanked by the hip stores of Karen Chekerdjian and Rabih Kayrouz-and then order a freshly crafted Mojito at nearby bistro Lux.
- Address: Abdel Azziz Street, Hamra
- Tel. 01-341 756

SHOP

05 *Johnny Farah

Johnny Farah has designed for Donna Karan, opened Beirut's coolest restaurants (including Casablanca, Lux and the now-closed Babylon) and constantly jets between Istanbul, New York, Paris and Montreal. His collection of leather goods reflects his travels. Simple, elegant, it comes in earthy tones with hand-stitched detailing. The belts and wallets are wonderful basics, the distressed messenger bags are chic enough for work and the silver chains and bracelets make perfect gifts.

Tip: Every Saturday morning you'll run into Johnny at Souk el Tayeb, the local farmers' market, where he sells herbs and vegetables grown in his mountain grove.
- Address: Said Akl Street, Saifi Village
- Tel. 01-974 808
- W.johnnyfarah.com

06 *Liwan

Whether it's to decorate an idyllic beach house somewhere remote, or to pick a gift for a special someone, Liwan, interior designer Lina Audi's Mar Mikhael boutique, has it all. Caftans, printed pillows, silk throws, leather sandals, belts and handmade soaps. There are also hand-beaded placemats and coasters and alabaster votives made from the salt of the Siwa Oasis. Everything is designed by Audi herself and crafted by the best local and regional artisans.

Tip: Liwan also has a very popular Paris branch.
- Address: Madrid Street, Mar Mikhael
- Tel. 01-444 141
- W.liwan.org

07 *Madame Rêve

A vintage-style necklace with pearls and brooches always adds a personal, sophisticated touch to a silk shirt or evening dress. At Madame Rêve, old cameos, pendants and ornaments are transformed into new jewels that are unique and poetic. The designers, Hala Mouzannar and Lina Chamaa, peruse markets and antique stores in Paris, Milan and London looking for unique vintage pieces. They then rework them, adding stones, pearls, precious Japanese silk ribbons and other baubles. The space, created by Architects Anonymous and inspired by Ingmar Bergman's Vertigo, is a surreal white room filled with jewelry-covered black mannequins.

Tip: Ask about the dOt collection, a series of jewels set with a "dot," or circular gem.
- Address: Gohlam Stairs, Mar Mikhael
- Tel. 01-565 545
- W.madamereve.net

08 *Nada Zeineh

For a thoughtful, delicate present visit jewelery designer Nada Zeineh's studio. Her cameos, brooches and earrings, dipped in gold using ancient Oriental textiles and pearls, are truly unique and luxurious. Zeineh draws from both her training as an architect and her experience in archeology to create Ottoman-inspired jewels that you'll be the only one wearing at your parties in London or New York.

Tip: The long double chain necklace with olive leaves in silver and gold is a classic.
- Address: 16 Sursock Street, Ashrafieh.
- Tel. 01-448 156

SHOP

09 *Orient 499

This stunning boutique is paradise for anyone who loves beautiful objects, spa products and clothes inspired by the Orient. Silk robes in jewel tones or traditional prints are light enough for travel and make for lovely gifts. Porcelain pomegranates are the perfect keepsakes. Oriental essences of amber, orange blossom and jasmine are of the highest quality. Linen towels and tablecloths are luxurious and modern. Frank Luca, the co-owner, also designs minimalist furniture with Middle Eastern motifs, such as wooden side tables inlaid with marqueterie. Objects come in adorable fabric bags embroidered with a gold bird, the store's mascot. No wonder Catherine Deneuve is a regular.

Tip: Take a look at the antique Oriental jewelry – it may be a bit costly, but chances are you will not find such rare pieces anywhere else.
  - **Address:** Omar Daouk Street, Mina el Hosn
  - **Tel.** 01-369 499
  - **W.**orient499.com

10 *Piaff

Piaff, an elegant boutique opened several decades ago by Salam Matouk and now run by her son Nabil al Houssami, sells the best brands for people who know their conceptual fashion. Beirut's curators and fashion entrepreneurs head there for Issey Miyake, Martin Grant, Hussein Chalayan and younger names like Mary Katranzou and Acne. The staff knows clients personally and advises them the way a personal stylist would.

Tip: The boutique keeps your birthdate in the system for special anniversary treats.
  - **Address:** Clemenceau Street, Clemenceau
  - **Tel.** 01-362 368 or 01-976 677 for Allenby Street
  - **W.**piaffboutique.com

11 *Plum

For all the girls who dream of cool young designers and their cute party dresses, there is Plum. This loft-like concept store is filled with handpicked pieces by Hakaan, Roland Mouret, Proenza Schouler and Preen. Shoe fanatics can also find their dose of Charlotte Olympia and Pierre Hardy pumps; for everyday chic Repetto ballerinas have lovely ranges of shades and prints. Top it all off with Tom Binns costume jewelry – just the right touch of punk.

Tip: The store also has an outlet where unsold pieces from summer and winter collections go for 50 percent off and more…
- Address: Park and Avenue Française, Downtown, Beirut
- Tel. 01-976 565
- W.plumconcept.com

12 *Rabih Kayrouz

Lebanon's most poetic couturier is now a member of the Chambre Syndicale de la Couture in Paris and an international star. He creates urban-inspired clothing with prêt-à-porter comfort and the tailoring and luxury of couture. Kayrouz became well-known in the nineties for his elaborate, ethereal wedding dresses; for many years he has dressed Arab royals such as Queen Rania of Jordan. Now his minimalist and colorful creations grace the pages of French Vogue and Elle; he welcomes in-the-know clients in both his Paris and Beirut ateliers.

Tip: At Kayrouz's new SoPo (South of the Port) boutique, take a look at Antwerp-trained jeweler Ed Thongprasert's surreal silicone gemstone necklaces. They come in sapphire, ruby and emerald tones and are either delicate enough for a sensual evening dress or chunky enough to brighten up a cotton shirtdress.
- Address: Darwish Haddad Street, Port of Beirut
- Tel. 01-444 221
- W.maisonrabihkayrouz.com

13 *Rosa Maria

Rosy Abourous grew up inspired by the antique jewels picked up by her parents on trips around the world. Soon she, too, began crafting rings with rough finishes and precious stones. Mixing silver, gold, zinc and topaz, rose-cut diamonds and sapphire. Her line, Rosa Maria, was soon picked up by IF boutique and L'Éclaireur in Paris, as well as numerous stores worldwide. Now Abourous has just opened a concept store in the up-and-coming Mar Mikhael area where, along with her jewels, she sells a personal selection of clothes and accessories such as Numero 10 leather bags, Officine Creative shoes, and Lost&Found scarves.

Tip: Rosie Abourous makes custom jewels for those looking for a very special piece.
- Address: 56, Madrid Street, Mar Mikhael
- Tel. 01-571 985
- W.rosamariajewellery.com

14 *Sarah's bag

Sociologist Sarah Beydoun founded this line as part of a rehabilitation program to help economically and socially deprived women. She works with artisans and previously incarcerated women who skillfully embroider silk purses, transform pop prints into clutches, and craft unique jewels and even iPad covers. In her beautiful boutique in Tabaris, there are arcade windows looking onto a quaint alleyway, birdcages and antique furniture.

Tip: If you've missed it this time around, the brand is also sold at Colette in Paris.
- Address: 100 Rue du Liban, Ashrafieh
- Tel. 01-575 585
- W.sarahsbag.com

15 *Starch Foundation

In the quaint Saifi Village, nested between the best Lebanese fashion stores, Starch showcases young Lebanese designers on a rotating basis. Launched in 2008 by couturier Rabih Kayrouz and Tala Hajjar with the support of Solidere, the Foundation picks four to six designers every year and helps them create and sell a full collection.

Tip: Several Starch 'graduates' now have their own store. Ask about them.
- Address: 1051 Quartier des Arts, Saifi
- Tel. 01-566 079
- W.starchfoundation.com

Necklace by Bird On A Wire

Daniel Abdel Sater

BOHO BEIRUT

FASHION DESIGNERS
THE UP-AND-COMERS

Beirut has a vibrant design scene, with young designers who create ornate evening dresses or conceptual urban uniforms. Here are some of my favorites:

Lara Khoury studied at French fashion school ESMOD, worked with Elie Saab and launched her eponymous collection in 2010. Her work is minimalist and feminine and impeccably cut; she loves the poetry of tulle and champagne silk. She is also launching a couture service soon for those who need something unique but not too traditional. (larakhoury.com) Krikor Jabotian is venerated for his lavish dresses adorned with rich embroideries, draped silks, sequins and ruffles: a wonderful choice for a very special occasion. (krikorjabotian.com) Karine Tawil, who has worked with Marni and Reem Acra, makes architecturally-inspired dresses in luxurious fabrics and vibrant colors – between couture and prêt-à-porter. (Karolinelang.com) Rayya Morcos' new Bird on a Wire label is both underground and classic, with beautiful silk prints and bright hues (she was previously a senior designer at Rabih Kayrouz). (birdonawireonline.com)

THE TASTEMAKERS

ROSIE ABO-U ROUS

THE DREAMER

HOW DOES BEIRUT INSPIRE YOU?

{ BEIRUT INSPIRES ME IN ALL HER ASPECTS:. NATURE, FOOD, FOUR SEASONS, CULTURE AND GOOD LIFE. I FIND IT MAGIC IN ALL HER UPS AND DOWNS. BEIRUT'S HEART IS ALWAYS BEATING. URBANISM AND LACK OF URBANISM, CHAOS AND LACK OF CHAOS . IT IS VERY CONTRASTING. HAPPINESS, LONELINESS, JOY OF LIFE, SADNESS, ALL THIS RESUME BEIRUT IN ONE WORD. }

BOHO BEIRUT

-125-

A GUIDE TO THE MIDDLE EAST'S MOST SOPHISTICATED...

SHOP

THE TASTEMAKERS:

ROSIE ABOU ROUS
The Dreamer

Rosie Abourous finds inspiration in a shell lying on a beach, a pomegranate or an ornate Ottoman brooch to create jewels that are earthy and luxurious. Her silver and gold rings are molded in rough shapes. Their rose-cut stones in deep tonalities – rubies, sapphires and diamonds are set randomly as if they, too, had been found on some luxuriant shore. They are designed to be stacked to create contrasts of shapes, textures and colors. Abourous, who sells her jewelry all over the world, including at L'Éclaireur, has recently opened her own boutique, Rosa Maria. In her earthy wooden boudoir, tobacco-leather club chairs, recycled iron fixtures and fine candles mingle with leatherware and accessories brands the jeweler handpicks from around the world.

YOUR FAVORITE LEBANESE DESIGNER?

I love Johnny Farah. His designs are very primitive and raw and rough. I also like Krikor Jabotian. His work is very detailed, precious, exuberant, and it's very stylish and sophisticated. His designs are thoroughly researched and inspired by vintage fashion. I always have nightgowns by Nadia Khoury – in off-white and embroidered.

YOUR FAVORITE RESTAURANT?

Casablanca is perfect for me because I'm a vegetarian. They have all sorts of seafood and salads; I love the raw fish and dumplings and the angel's hair with light sauces – or decadent botarga.

A NICE COFFEE SHOP?

I like Papercup; I find it beautiful and cozy and there's always a book that appeals to me. I love the way they serve the tea and the homemade cakes.

WHERE DO YOU RELAX?

I go in to the Rabieh Marine Hotel. It's in the middle of nowhere: there's no one there. I swim a lot and when the sea is rough I like to ride the waves.

BEST LEBANESE AUTHOR?

I love Amin Maalouf's *Le Rocher de Tanious*

AN INTERIOR DESIGNER?

Karim Chaya's furniture is very rough, which fits my esthetic.

A GUIDE TO THE MIDDLE EAST'S MOST SOPHISTICATED CITY

SHOP

JOHNNY FARAH
SAID AKL STREET, SAIFI VILLAGE
TEL. 01-974 808
W.JOHNNYFARAH.COM
KRIKOR JABOTIAN
DAKDOUK BUILDING, SELIM BUSTROS STREET, TABARIS
TEL. 01-204 793
W.KRIKORJABOTIAN.COM
NADIA KHOURY
CORNICHE, AIN EL MREISSEH
W.ARTISANSDULIBAN.COM
TEL. 01-362 610
CASABLANCA
DAR EL-MREISSEH STREET, AIN EL-MREISSEH
TEL. 01-369 334
PAPER CUP
AGOPIAN BUILDING, PHARAON STREET, MAR MIKHAEL
TEL. 01-443 083
W.PAPERCUPSTORE.COM

RABIYA MARINE HOTEL
SAFRA, JOUNIEH
TEL. 09-854 777
W.RABIYAMARINE.COM
KARIM CHAYAA
TEL. 04-542 007
W.ACID-WORKS.COM

A GUIDE TO THE MIDDLE EAST'S MOST SOPHISTICATED CITY

~~ADDRESS~~ BOOK
ROSIE ABOU ROUS

SHOP

THE TASTEMAKERS

TALA HAJJAR

THE COMMUNICATOR

HOW DOES BEIRUT INSPIRE YOU?

{ THE LUMINOSITY AND COLORS WITH THE CHANGE OF SEASONS. MAY AND OCTOBER ARE MY FAVORITE MONTHS FOR THE CLEAREST BLUE SKIES. SIT IN THE SUN, CLOSE YOUR EYES AS YOU TAKE A DEEP BREATH. }

BOHO BEIRUT

-131-

A GUIDE TO THE MIDDLE EAST'S MOST SOPHISTICATED CITY

SHOP

THE TASTEMAKERS:

TALA HAJJAR
The Communicator

With her lithe silhouette, long straw-colored mane and avant-garde wardrobe, Tala Hajjar is Beirut's own "it"girl – and she's also making her mark in the fashion industry. Hajjar, who studied at Central St. Martins and worked with couturier Rabih Kayrouz for three years, is now at the helm of Starch, an initiative to support budding designers. Founded by Solidere, Kayrouz and Hajjar, Starch chooses four to six designers each year and helps them create a collection step-by-step. They are also invited to exhibit and sell their clothes at the elegant Starch store in Saifi village. Meetings with couturiers and fashion experts from around the world help budding talents understand the stakes of the industry. Hajjar won the Young Entrepreneur Award from the British Council. Clearly, it's only a start for the globe-trotting entrepreneur.

FAVORITE JEWELLER?
Although she has been featured in Italian Vogue and won her "Best Newcomer" at London Jewelry Week in 2010, Joanna Dahdah is still very much under the radar. Her store, designed by cool architecture studio APractice, sells her own collections along with handpicked international designers.

BEST SPOT FOR GIFTS?
Rouba Mourtada's stationery, Choux à la Crème, is modern and pretty. By appointment.

FAVORITE YOUNG DESIGNER?
The brand, Ashekman Urban Wear was established by graffiti artists Mohamed and Omar Kabbani, who combine their graphic design studies and passion for hip-hop to create a distinctly Lebanese clothing line. Their T-shirts mix Arabic graffiti, urban graphics, calligraphy and Lebanese proverbs.

BEST-KEPT SECRET?
Rana Salam. After years in London, where she created displays for Harvey Nichols and concepts for Paul Smith, Rana opened a Beirut showroom for her kitschy Lebanese posters, prints, wall art, stationery, textiles and furnishings. She is also the co-author of the naughty book, *The Secret Life of Syrian Lingerie.*

A GUIDE TO THE MIDDLE EAST'S MOST SOPHISTICATED CITY

JOANNA DAHDAH
HERMITAGE BUILDING ASHRAFIEH
TEL. 03-574 945
W.JOANNADAHDAH.COM
CHOUX À LA CRÈME
CLEMENCEAU STREET, RAS BEIRUT
TEL. 03-889 622
W.CHOUXALACREME.COM
ASHEKMAN URBAN WEAR
HAMRA STREET, HAMRA
TEL. 01-739 598
W.ASHEKWAN.COM
RANA SALAM
RIZK BUILDING ASHRAFIEH
TEL. 01-217 244
W.MISHMAOUL.COM

ADDRESS BOOK

TALA HAJJAR

A GUIDE TO THE MIDDLE EAST'S MOST SOPHISTICATED CITY

SHOP

S&T

STAY/*TIPS*

Visitors never forget the Lebanese's legendary hospitality. For locals it's a matter of honor to treat one's guest to the finest foods and luxuries and to show them a memorable time. As most Lebanese are convinced that their country is the most beautiful in the world, they are eager to convert tourists, too, to their unconditional love. Of course, the critical traveler must disregard the general chaos, pollution, insane traffic and deep corruption that plague the country. Once the adjustment is made, Lebanon's charms emerge. Getting lost is not an issue here, as it's common practice to paralyze the traffic and ask for directions. When walking into someone's home, one is overwhelmed with offers of food, drinks and gifts. Men are charming and flirtatious, and women spend their days complimenting each other (although we could certainly question their full sincerity.) At the beach, a regimen of waiters caters to your every need, from an ice-cold beer to carrots and lemon, fresh watermelon and a pack of cigarettes. Ahhh, those rare luxuries! In Lebanon service is very good and generally inexpensive, from personal chefs to beauty pros, dedicated chauffeurs, caterers and domestic help. As far as hotels are concerned there are few options between the very high-end (the Phoenicia and Four Seasons are a bit too bling) and the very low-end (backpackers b&bs), but now new cool hotels and rentals are opening in the city for those looking for stylish and affordable alternatives.

A GUIDE TO THE MIDDLE EAST'S MOST SOPHISTICATED CITY

01 *Albergo

This Relais et Châteaux hotel is a home away from home for sophisticated travelers. The quaint lobby, decorated by Jacques Garcia in an ornate Old World style, is scented with antique rose perfume. Here, every detail counts: There are tiled floors, marqueterie wood cupboards, beaded chandeliers and fresh flowers everywhere. Each room is decorated in a unique style. The restaurant is filled with Oriental antiques and paintings, and the luxuriant plants create an exotic atmosphere. Food is also served on the rooftop, where the hotel's legendary brunch, which includes *zaatar* breads and fig jam, is served on summer days.

Tip: The suites have splendid terrace gardens.
- Address: Abdel Wahab el Inglizi Street, Ashrafieh
- Tel. 01-339 797
- W.albergobeirut.com

02 *Beirut Nests

After a holiday at a guesthouse in the United States in 1995, Fabienne Ziadé, who has worked in banking, radio and diplomacy, decided to open her own rental apartments in her hometown. Now she manages nine spaces throughout the city, including several downtown, and guestrooms in Ashrafieh apartments. The apartments are clean, comfortable, and nicely decorated – the Mar Mikhael studio is especially centrally located.

Tip: The company offers special prices for long-term stays.
- Tel. 03-835 849
- W.beirutnests.com

BOHO BEIRUT

03 *Hayete Guest House

This lovely b&b in Tabaris is owned by Simone Tengel, a Swiss lady who has fallen for the charms of Beirut. She has decorated an old Lebanese house with antiques from the Basta flea market and named it Hayete, literally "my life," but colloquially meaning "my love." There are four rooms with beautiful tiled floors, and in the charming lobby, a bar and a birdcage. Here the atmosphere is relaxed and friendly; you can even request an in-room manicure and pedicure.

Tip: Parking is impossible in this area, so let the valet take care of your car.
- **Address:** Bashir Gemayel Street, Ashrafieh
- **Tel.** 01-331 530 / 03-948 918
- **W.**hayete-guesthouse.com

04 *Le Gray

Centrally located in downtown Beirut, near the Beirut Souks, Le Gray is an elegant and convenient place to stay. Filled with art works handpicked by Gordon Campbell, the owner, the hotel offers 87 luxurious rooms with REN beauty products, Porthault linen, Wi-Fi and an iPod dock. Each day fresh flowers and fruits are delivered to the rooms. The hotel also has a rooftop pool prized by the city's beautiful people, with a panoramic view of the country's mountains and coast. For meetings there are two restaurants and a cigar room. The 360 bar, with its panoramic view, live concerts and fun cocktails, is one of the best rooftop bars in town.

Tip: Also check in at the spa, a Zen haven offering relaxing and rejuvenating massages, and follow with a "brushing" at the hair salon.
- **Address:** Martyrs' Square, Beirut Central District
- **Tel.** 01-971 111
- **W.**campbellgrayhotels.com

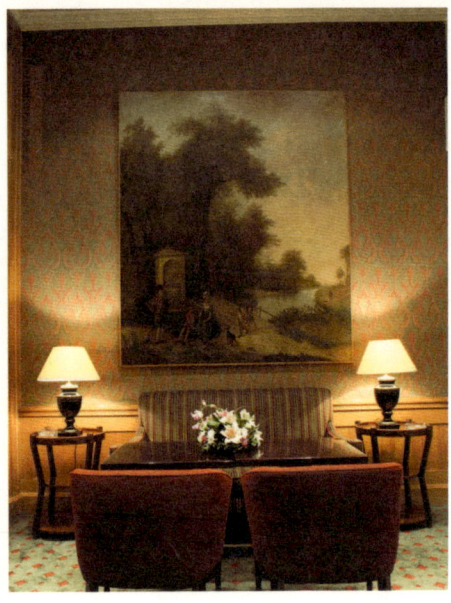

05 *Saifi Urban Gardens

Saifi Urban Gardens is a fun oasis in the middle of Beirut, with a garden, outdoor sculptures, a restaurant (Em Nazih) and a rooftop bar (Coop d'Etat). The building is also the home of the Saifi Institute for Arabic Language and room rentals are as cheap as $15 a night. That's for dorm style, of course, but if you need more privacy you get your own room with en-suite bathroom.

Tip: Busy travelers can sign up for a private Arabic crash course.
- Address : Pasteur Street, Gemmayze
- Tel. 01-562 509
- W.saifigardens.com

06 *Sofitel Le Gabriel

Le Gabriel is a sophisticated business hotel. Decorated in a classic French style, the hotel offers 74 rooms, including eight deluxe suites and one presidential suite. The elevators are painted in lovely garden murals, and in the summer guests can dine in a sunny garden adjacent to the restaurant. The business center accommodates meetings and conferences.

Tip: The hotel has a full gym, swimming pool, sauna/steam bath and spa for health buffs.
- Address: Independence Ave., Ashrafieh
- Tel. 01-203 700
- W.sofitel.com

BOHO BEIRUT

07 *Villa Clara*

Olivier Gougeon studied hotel and restaurant management in Paris and inaugurated Aziz's restaurant and Balima in Beirut and Edde Yards restaurant in Byblos. When he found a house dating from 1910 and surrounded with a lush garden in Mar Mikhael, he decided to convert it into a hotel: Villa Clara. He decorated the rooms with the antiquities having the mystique of the Hotel St. James in Paris, including the Andrée Putman room. We like the tiny prices, a rarity in this city. In the lobby and garden, the restaurant serves fresh French cuisine with produce grown on the hotel's rooftop and on the mountain orchard Gougeon owns.

Tip: At the restaurant Gougeon serves dishes "sur mesure," so dream up your perfect combination and request it from the chef.
- Address: Khanshara Street, Mar Mikhael
- Tel. 70-995 739

T
TIPS

01 *Bike rental

With its hysterical drivers, inexistent street codes and narrow streets, Beirut is not exactly a bike-friendly city. But for those who want to take the risk, or bike on friendlier territory such as the Corniche and the countryside, Beirut by Bike has two central renting spots and offers biking advice, too. It also organizes tailored events around the country.

Tip: Ask about the Beirut by Segway tours- a fun way to discover the city.
- Address: Graham Street, Ain Mreisseh
- Tel: 01-365 524
- W.beirutbybike.com

02 *Hairdresser

Ask any socialite or businessman where they get their hair done, and they invariably mention Kan. After years in Paris, this bubbly stylist opened his own salon in Ashrafieh, Kan Paris, where he gives clients modern, layered cuts and natural colors that look glamorous and effortless.

Tip: There is also an in-house manicurist and makeup artist for pre-party prep.
- Address: Zahret el Ihsan Street, Ashrafieh
- Tel. 01-328 666

03 *Massage

We hear that Kai at Jacques Dessange is the best masseuse in the country. In a bare massage room, she stretches and pulls every limb and muscle in the true Thai massage tradition.

Tip: For a quick fix to your messy hair, book a brushing with hairstylist Nizar in the Dessange hair salon downstairs.
- **Address: Furn el Hayeck Street, Ashrafieh**
- **Tel: 01-325 503**
- **W.dessange-lb.com**

04 *Taxis

There's no reliable public transportation in Beirut, so if you haven't rented a car (or if you plan to have a particularly crazy night), taxis are essential. Many people hop in the shared "service" taxis during the day (about 2$ per rider) but at night calling a car service is recommended. Allô taxi is the most popular company, but for extra thrills London Taxi's British-style cars are fun.

Tip: Plan ahead as most taxis need at least half an hour to an hour to arrive.
- **Tel. 1213 (Allô Taxi)**
- **Tel. 09-857 300 (London Taxi)**

THE TASTEMAKERS

GORDON CAMPBELL -
THE GLOBETROTTER

HOW DOES BEIRUT INSPIRE YOU?

{ THE UNDERPINNING IS THE COMPLETE DESIRE OF PEOPLE TO REALLY LIVE EVERY DAY FOR THE DAY. WHEN I LAND IN BEIRUT IT REALLY LIFTS MY SPIRITS. }

-145-

THE TASTEMAKERS:

GORDON CAMPBELL
The globetrotter

The Galapagos, London, Mumbai, Caracas, Bogota, Palm Beach. Hotelier Gordon Campbell wanders the world for work and pleasure, opening hotels such as Beirut's Le Gray. And though Campbell, who is Scottish, calls London his home, he also has a pied-à-terre in Beirut's Saifi Village. "Beirut and London are two marvelous cities to live in," he muses. "They offer different things. In London we have culture and art and order and then you go to Beirut and throw the order out the window and you live everyday. I like the freedom of living there and I love the weather." Campbell likes to walk around Beirut, a rare activity in this car-centered city. He enjoys days at the beach, entertaining and visiting the city's many galleries to purchase art works. His acquisitions often find their way into his hotel, adding his personal touch to the sleek contemporary décor.

BEST RESTAURANTS?

I love Tawlet. The ethos of what Kamal Mouzawak does there – supporting local agriculture and culinary traditions – is really good. I go to Margherita on the nights when I just feel like a pizza.

WHERE DO YOU GO FOR A DRINK?

I love Prague. When I'm there I feel like I should be plotting a revolution. It has great music, it's divvy, very kind of Chelsea. In Gemmayze my favorite place is Dragonfly. I always have the same thing there a perfect Manhattan. They just pour it in whenever they see me.

WHERE DO YOU PICK UP GIFTS?

I usually buy people paintings, as I love art. Some of the city's best galleries are Agial, Janine Rubeiz and Sfeir-Semler.

BEACH GETAWAYS?

I like going to Lazy B; it's very peaceful and not too pretentious. I like to tan and swim in the sea. In Batroun I like the restaurant Jamal for seafood. It's literally a feet in the water experience.

A GUIDE TO THE MIDDLE EAST'S MOST SOPHISTICATED CITY

TAWLET
CHALHOUB BUILDING, NAHR STREET, MAR MIKHAEL
TEL. 01-448 129
W.TAWLET.COM

MARGHERITA
GOURAUD STREET, GEMMAYZE
TEL. 01-560 480
W.PIZZERIAMARGHERITA.COM

DE PRAGUE
MAKDESSI STREET, HAMRA
TEL. 01-744 864

DRAGONFLY
GOURAUD STREET, GEMMAYZE
TEL. 01-561 112

AGIAL
63 ABDUL AZIZ STREET, HAMRA
TEL. 01-345 213

JANINE RUBEIZ
MAJDALANI BUILDING, 1 CHARLES DE GAULLE AVENUE, RAOUCHE
TEL. 01-868 290
W.GALERIEJANINERUBEIZ.COM

SFEIR-SEMLER
TANNOUS BUILDING, KARANTINA
TEL. 01-566 550
W.SFEIR-SEMLER.DE
LAZY B
JIYEH
TEL. 70-950 010
W.LAZYB.ME
JAMMAL
KFARABIDA, BATROUN
TEL. 06-740 095

A GUIDE TO THE MIDDLE EAST'S MOST SOPHISTICATED CITY

~~ADDRESS~~ BOOK
GORDON CAMPBELL

S&T

THE TASTEMAKERS

OLIVIER GE-MAYEL
THE MA-GICIAN

HOW DOES BEIRUT INSPIRE YOU?

{ BEIRUT INSPIRES ME BECAUSE OF ITS UNIQUENESS AND CULTURAL DIVERSITY. IT ALSO HAS CHALLENGING OBSTACLES, WHICH MAKES ACHIEVING ONE'S GOALS SO MUCH MORE REWARDING. }

BOHO BEIRUT

-151-

A GUIDE TO THE MIDDLE EAST'S MOST SOPHISTICATED CITY

THE TASTEMAKERS:

OLIVIER GEMAYEL
The magician

Concierge Olivier Gemayel has rented a pink jet for one client's daughter's eighteenth birthday bash. He has organized a romantic dinner in Versailles mirror gallery for a couple. He has booked Madonna and Elton John for private concerts. He has thrown an intimate party with a Lebanese star at the Beirut National Museum. This exceptional service has earned him a Clef d'Or, a prestigious distinction reserved for the best concierges in the world. After stints in Paris, where he studied hospitality and worked at Fouquet's; New York, where he learned a few tricks with Alain Ducasse and London; where he started his personal concierge company, Gemayel is now back in Beirut. His new project, SS Signature, offers to take care of his clients' most minute needs – from tours to high dining, couture, adventure and even chores like food shopping. Gemayel has partnered with Saradar Bank to create this highly personalized venture where activities are divided in three categories: Everyday Life, Leisure Life and Exceptional Life. Gemayel also organizes tours of Beirut with historians.

BEST RESTAURANTS?
I love organizing dinners at chef Hussein Hadid's home. It's very beautiful and you can eat in the large kitchen while you watch him cook sophisticated, Arab-inspired dishes. Hadid is known as the star caterer of the country.

DRINKS?
I enjoy having a drink at the bar at Momo, which becomes a nightclub at night. Torino Express has the best cocktails in Beirut.

BEACH?
I love the Sporting, which has kept its beach authentic and simple. The view of Pigeons' Rock and the horizon is priceless.

SPAS?
The Shiseido Spa in Ashrafieh is a true haven, with real shiatsu and Thai massage. G Spa is also very Zen and relaxing.

DRIVER?
Elvis Taxi is mythical: He has the Elvis figurine, the blasting music, the retro haircut and even the sunglasses!

HUSSEIN HADID
MAR ELIAS
TEL. 01-816 120
W.HUSSEINHADID.COM
MOMO
BEIRUT SOUKS, DOWNTOWN
TEL. 01-999 767
W.MOMORESTO.COM
TORINO EXPRESS
GOURAUD STREET, GEMMAYZE
TEL. 03-611 101
SPORTING
CORNICHE EL-MANARA
TEL. 01-742 484
SHISEIDO SPA
ELIAS SARKIS AVENUE, ASHRAFIEH
TEL. 01-332 277
W.SHISEIDOSPAS.COM

GSPA
INDEPENDENCE AVENUE, ASHRAFIEH
TEL. 01-210 220
W.GSPA.COM
ELVIS TAXI
RUE DU LIBAN
TEL. 03-494 939

~~ADDRESS~~
BOOK OLIVIER GEMAYEL

A GUIDE TO THE MIDDLE EAST'S MOST SOPHISTICATED CITY

Se

SUMMER *ESCAPE*

Ask the Lebanese what their favorite activity is and they'll invariably mention eating or lazing at the beach. With at least five months of clear blue skies, warm sea water and radiant sun, the shores of Lebanon are assaulted all summer by amateurs of coconut oil, watersports and fishing. Avoid public beaches, which tend to be dirty and unsafe; some private beaches feel closer to tacky nightclubs. Local favorites are in Beirut, Jiyyeh, in the south, or Batroun, in the north.

A GUIDE TO THE MIDDLE EAST'S MOST SOPHISTICATED CITY

Lazy B

01 *Lazy B

For a long, luxuriant day at the beach, Beirutis head to Lazy B in the southern coastal town of Jiyyeh. Straw huts and wooden day beds offer private havens throughout the grassy hills that lead up to the sandy beach. Those who want to mingle gather around the two swimming pools or at the restaurant.

Tip: Treat yourself to a massage in a quiet cabana.
- Address: Jiyyeh
- W.lazyb.me

02 *Le Gray

Le Gray's infinity swimming pool is quiet and private, and offers 360° views of the city and horizon. It's near the restaurant and café, and for a healthy fix, fresh juices are served poolside.

Tip: We think a massage at the spa is just the perfect ending to a relaxing day in the sun.
- Address: Martyrs' Square, Beirut Central District
- Tel. 01-971 111
- W.campbellgreyhotels.com

03 *Sporting Club

In the heart of Beirut, this unassuming concrete beach is a perennial classic for old schoolers and artists. Some have been tanning or fishing daily on its plastic lounge chairs for decades, facing the legendary Pigeons' Rock and smoking Marlboro Lights. Beware of weekend crowds.

Tip: The restaurant serves fresh fish and salads for a mid-afternoon snack.
- Address: Chouran Street, El-Manara
- Tel. 01-742 481

04 *St. Georges

When Beirut was glamorous, most of its social gatherings happened at the St. Georges. This is where the beauties of the pre-war days continue to brown their skin with the help of baby oil, Almaza beers and Winston cigarettes.

Tip: St. Georges now faces the Zaitunay Bay promenade, so beware of passers-by peeping in.
- Address: Ain Mreisseh
- Tel. 01-958 376
- W.stgeorges-yachtclub.com

~~THINGS TO~~ KNOW

~~CURRENCY~~
Here the currencies are the US dollar and the Lebanese pound. One US dollar equals 1,500 LL. Always keep both currencies with you and keep in mind that ATM machines are around, but you never know when they might run short on dispensing cash.

~~IMPORTANT NUMBERS~~
Airport: 01-628 000
Civil Defense: 125
Police: 160
Tourist Police: 01-350 901
International operator: 100
Red Cross: 140
Population of Lebanon: 3.8 million (2009) (excluding 222,776 Palestinians living in refugee camps)

~~NEWS~~
The English-language daily is *The Daily Star*, an excellent newspaper with a comprehensive arts section.

~~ESSENTIAL READING~~
Samir Kassir: *Beirut*
Written by Lebanon's most prominent intellectual shortly before his tragic death, this book offers a comprehensive history of the country through 5,000 years of successive empires and wars.

Annia Ciezadlo: *Day of Honey: A Memoir of Food, Love and War*
This beautifully written book covers politics, culture and food – the Lebanese's favorite subjects – with wit, humor and poetry.

Amin Maalouf: *The Rock of Tanios*
Amin Maalouf is Lebanon's best-known writer, and he is a member of the Académie Française. *The Rock of Tanios* describes the conflict-ridden Lebanon of the 1980s through the story of Tanios, a mountain boy.

A GUIDE TO THE MIDDLE EAST'S MOST SOPHISTICATED CITY

BOHO BEIRUT

PLAN OF BEIRUT.

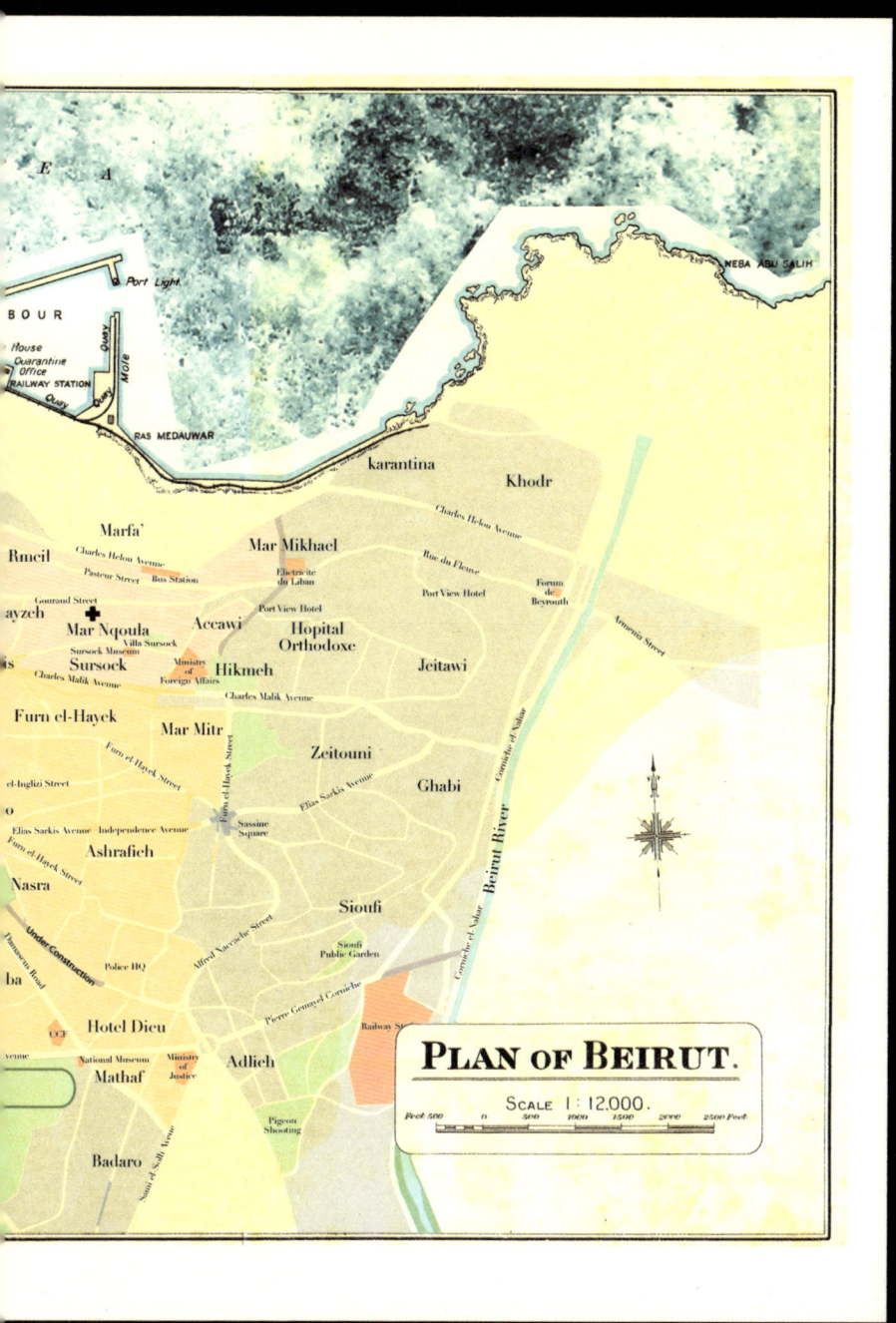

A GUIDE TO THE MIDDLE EAST'S MOST SOPHISTICATED CITY

MAP